CORE SELF THEORY

CORE SELF
THEORY

Discovering Self-Acceptance
and
How to Live Authentically

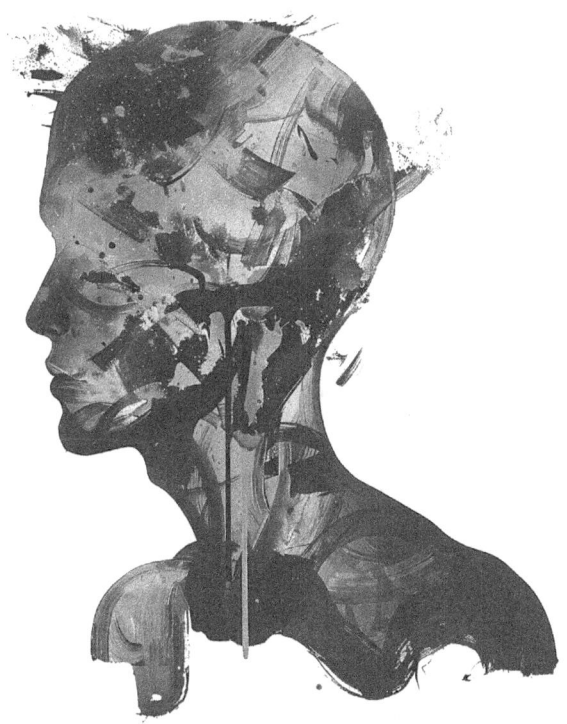

Dr. John S. Saroyan

TRANSFORMATION MEDIA BOOKS
Saint Louis, Missouri

Published by Transformation Media Books, USA

TRANSFORMATION
MEDIA BOOKS

www.TransformationMediaBooks.com
info@TransformationMediaBooks.com

An imprint of Pen & Publish, LLC
Saint Louis, Missouri
(314) 827-6567
www.PenandPublish.com

Paperback ISBN: 978-1-956897-60-9
ebook ISBN: 978-1-956897-61-6
Library of Congress Control Number: 2025934034

Credit for Figure 5: M. W. Toews
Credit for Figure 4: based on figure by M. W. Toews

I dedicate this book to my beautiful wife, Gladys, who is as real and honest as they come. Thank you for listening to my conceptual ideas as I was developing this book and for the countless discussions we shared on this subject during our times together, whether at home or during our long and numerous drives.

Contents

Preface

Welcome to Core Self Theory. This is a model of psychology that focuses on the Self, *your* Self. Through my experience as a Clinical Psychologist and Marriage and Family Therapist, I have explored several theories of personality that were developed and studied by prominent psychiatrists and psychologists. I have also explored separate or accompanying treatment modalities presented by other well-known master clinicians. Most treatment approaches have their place for working with clients. They use specific communication styles or approaches, as well as interventions that are useful when helping clients overcome personal problems and resolve interpersonal struggles. Most psychotherapists have adopted a certain theoretical model that corresponds with their specific treatment approaches. These clinicians recognize that they have had treatment successes that may ultimately reinforce their repeated approaches to therapy, even when populations may vary or not respond as anticipated.

Through the years, I have recognized the value of having the flexibility to change my therapeutic approach and adapt to clients' needs by using best practices in treatment models as they relate to a particular client. No two clients are the same, and neither can their symptoms be exactly the same. For instance, one man or one woman's depression may vary in terms of intensity, frequency of episodes, or symptomatology. The symptoms of one person may be quite different from those of another, yet they are still classified with the same diagnosis of depression. This example is used to emphasize the uniqueness of each individual and how important it is to see the client as a separate being from all others, albeit certain personality traits may be common or familiar among the clients of a therapist. The important consideration here is that even though people can share similar personality characteristics, the whole of the person is unique. Each person is born with the genetics of both their parents' histories, which create a human who is completely distinct and special as an individual.

While reflecting on my training as a therapist, I found that there was an emphasis in adopting a theoretical orientation for the treatment of all clinical issues. It was common to hear fellow students claim that they were "eclectic" in their treatment approaches, yet eclecticism was not a theoretical orientation nor was it an acceptable "treatment modality." This was especially true with the Board of Examiners, who tested myself and other qualifying interns during oral examinations for state licensure. Interns grappled with questions such as, Which therapeutic model seemed right? What worked best for clients? How skilled am I in using these interventions? For me, it came down to being myself and then finding the clinical approach that fit my personality. I was fortunate to find the closest fit of Systems Theory using Structural and Strategic approaches. But over time, I embraced the freedom that some of my peers from graduate school experienced. I too was "eclectic" and could change my approach to best care for the clients I treated with emotional and behavioral struggles.

Adapting to my client was important. The ability to see and accept a client's uniqueness was one of the first skills I explored from my first class on the first day of graduate school. I understood that I needed to relate to my clients based on their temperament and personality. Once I could relate to the client, I strived to select the best treatment approach(es) that closely matched and related to their Self. I usually did not limit myself to one approach, since different approaches might be best depending on the focus of treatment or the need that was presented. The primary goal was to help someone be happier in their life. I resisted becoming boxed-in to a counseling model that was not working or that may alienate the client from therapy since they might not feel understood as the unique person that they are.

A person's uniqueness can be seen from infancy. Research shows that personality traits appearing early in one's life can still be identified later for that person during adulthood. Our environment also contributes to our personality development and cannot be discounted as a significant part of our growth. However, our innate Self and temperament style are the principal aspects of personality development that are discussed in this model. Traits do combine with life experiences, contributing to who we are. Since each one of us is born with unique genetics, and we all have different personal life histories and social experiences, no two humans have ever, or will ever, be the same. It is impossible.

Core Self Theory is a model that I have developed to help us understand ourselves and each other as unique human beings. The Core Self is that deep inner self that is within us and is always present. Those who understand their inner selves, can then interact better within their environment and not feel stuck within a paradigm constructed by others. When we can be our Core Self in the presence of others, we are choosing to be free, as ourselves, while not feeling obligated to accept the social standards set by others. When we are our Core Self, we are congruent with our own thoughts and feelings while not imposing these on anyone else. It is what happens when a person is true to themself through honest self-expression. It is an ability to acknowledge that a person's internal reactions are truly theirs and they have the freedom to express themself genuinely.

Core Self Theory has different applications with a common goal that is reality based. As a personal model, it can be utilized by anyone in their quest to understand themself and learn self-acceptance. From a social perspective, it influences our understanding, compassion, and acceptance for other people's uniquenesses. Therapeutically, counselors may use the principles of this model to guide clients toward deeper insight with greater awareness of actuality and truth, rather than typical expectations that become social norms yet are out of sync with one's Core Self.

Core Self Theory and the understanding of our Core Self is an original therapeutic approach that I have developed during my years as an educator, consultant, and mental health clinician. I must also give credit to other educators, researchers, and theorists who have influenced me through a humanistic background of counseling and personality development. Conceptual ideas related to personality formation are theoretical, however, much of what is presented can be supported through researched aspects of certain theoretical models that are shared. The common thread with these and other humanistic models is acceptance of individuality—for self and others.

Introduction

Core Self Theory is a model that emphasizes the importance of understanding one's inner self and accepting one's uniqueness that is present at all times. It is intended to promote personal growth and to increase social understanding. When we are able to conduct our lives as our Core Selves, we become free to *be* ourselves and interact authentically with others.

The development of Core Self Theory was initially influenced by different treatment modalities, as well as various theories of personality. Important theorists who have shaped my thoughts through the evolution of this model are Carl Rogers, with his trademark of Person-Centered Therapy, and Alfred Adler, a well-known proponent of Individual Psychology. Though there are several other theoreticians and researchers who have also influenced the creation of this model, much of what is presented in this book is original and based on my several years of experience as a psychotherapist.

Central principles of this model are built on the idea that each person is an individual with a unique set of experiences and traits that are influenced by a deeper part of the self. This deeper part of the self will be referred to as our Core Self. It is present at birth and remains with us throughout all our developmental stages. The two primary components of the Core Self are our temperament along with our inherent nature with a distinctive essence. These factors contribute to our personality development and shape who we are as individuals. When we understand our Core Selves, we can better recognize our motivations and behaviors, and we can make choices that ultimately correspond more accurately with our true selves.

This model also explores different levels of authenticity in terms of being our Core Self. As individuals we may struggle to openly or honestly think and behave in ways that are authentic to our true selves. When this conflict occurs, we are not being aligned with our Core Self. This can create feelings of anxiety or depression due to the incongruity between our Real Self and a Self that is Hidden or Lost. What is important is to discover our real authentic Self and consciously choose what parts of ourselves we can comfortably and appropriately share with the world around us.

The model presents a clear background to understanding the factors contributing to our Core Self and its connection to personality development. The model further explores the different Self types that will help guide the reader toward their choice of a personal presentation to others in their social interactions. Additional areas explored are self-acceptance, human variability, and the distancing from the Self as a form of Core Self denial. Within the chapters, I have presented several vignettes that will further explore topic discussions and will help clarify the issues reviewed.

Core Self Theory has a number of applications. Overall, this theoretical model can be useful when working on personal growth, social understanding, and therapeutic healing. On a personal level, it can help people understand themselves better as well as make decisions that are aligned with their true selves. On a social level, it can help people to develop healthier relationships and to be more effective in their interactions with others. Core Self Theory can help in understanding and acceptance of others. It can also lead to creating a more tolerant and inclusive society.

Therapy can be an effective way to explore Core Self Theory and to develop a deeper understanding of oneself. A therapist can help to facilitate the process of self-discovery and can provide support and guidance as you, the reader, learn to live more authentically.

There is no deeper desire than the desire of being revealed.

—Kahlil Gibran

Chapter 1

Individual Uniqueness

When I was a four-year-old child, I remember playing on the short, sloped driveway at my neighbor's house, waiting for their children to come out and play. I was bored during the wait and began poking around the plants and objects surrounding their driveway. I recall at one point slipping in a manner that dropped me to the slanted cement ground. During this fall, I skinned my knee. It was definitely not a superficial scrape, since it went below the epidermis and into the middle layer of skin. I recall the stinging pain highlighted by the progressive color transformation as I watched the scrape quickly turn from a normal flesh-colored hue, to pink, and then red blood. I remember crying from the physical pain as I worked my way back home with the intention of receiving my mother's care. Care not only meant the process of getting cleaned up and having a bandage to cover the injured sore; it also meant emotional care that could include loving and understanding for the pain I was experiencing, along with kind, supportive words of encouragement.

At this stage in my life, the emotional reaction to my injury was genuine. I was really hurting, and crying made sense. My helpless feelings were accompanied by physical pain that resulted in verbal emotional expression. Granted, I was just a child and the stinging shock from a skinned knee must have really hurt, but I was actually a normal little guy who fell a lot and got cuts and bruises all the time. This fall and injury felt different. Though I do not remember all those previous falling experiences, I know from seeing other children, as well as raising my own, that my four-year-old response was in line with the typical reaction of other children at that age who get hurt that way.

The questions coming to mind are, How would I have behaved under the same circumstances at age seven? What about my reaction to the same fall as a ten-year-old? Physically, pain signals still reach our brain, but they are at different levels of intensity for adults when compared to those for children. However, pain from the injury would still exist at any age. Accompanying emotions further add to the overall negative experience, but these feelings should also change with age. Though the degree of pain and the manner of expression of an adult would be less than that of a four-year-old child, something else is happening that ultimately modifies the reflex of expression and cognitively alters communication, becoming something foreign to the person. While pain receptors might gradually change from a high degree of sensitivity to a lesser degree over time (from childhood to adulthood), there are still overall psychosocial experiences that may carry an impact on individual behavior. Certain group rules and other social influences may reshape our natural reactions, thus creating new actions that are not consistent with our Real Self.

I believe my reaction to this falling incident was purely genuine. I injured my knee and it was stinging badly. As a four-year-old child, I was not aware of my neighbors who might have seen the fall. Physical care along with my emotional need for an attentive mother were the only things wanted at that moment in time. Reacting to the pain, as I immediately did, tells me how I was not concerned with neighborhood or peer judgments, since I cried all the way to my home. I was expressive and did not deny my pain. Had this event occurred a couple of years later, I might have been more concerned about being labeled a sissy or weak by my neighborhood friends. Also, I would have probably downplayed my pain in order to avoid parental worry. I would not want restrictions that would prevent me from having freedom to play unattended among friends.

At the risk of sounding accident prone, I can recall another fall. This one was at age eight while at school in the early morning. While playing among a group of friends, I fell from a wall and landed flat on my stomach with my chin hitting the concrete ground. The fall had knocked the wind out of me, and the immediate physical pain was significant. I remember pulling myself up to shake off the pain while hiding the discomfort of losing my breath. As I turned away, none of the other boys reacted to my fall, so I hid my painful experience. I would have felt embarrassed or humiliated had I stayed on the ground or stood bent over while whining from the hurt and pain I was feeling.

Had this same event occurred a few years earlier, I might have revealed the real, honest pain experienced. Instead, I hid it, avoiding probable ridicule from the guys in the group. A label as a supposed weakling could become part of my reputation, and I could not accept that. With this at stake, I hid and minimized my distress. I endured the pain. Though I was still hurting like the little four-year-old with a skinned knee, I was also aware that there could be negative judgments by my peer social group. Instead of expressing my physical pain, I internally worried about outwardly showing what I felt. This incongruent behavior forced me to withhold genuine emotions and left me feeling alone. I was alone because I had to maneuver this experience by myself, not having the option of turning to a maternal figure for comfort and understanding. Instead, I played the role of an independent and strong male who could handle tough physical situations. Remember, boys don't cry.

As we grow older, we encounter various hurtful and painful experiences. Some of our ability to withstand upsetting types of distress or discomfort comes from maturity. Life experiences as well as personal insights and understandings may lessen the feelings that we might have expressed early in our life or at a first encounter. Another consideration is that most of us learn social norms from our group affiliations and culture. The idea that one can express pain as a four-year-old but not an eight-year-old is more related to following social standards or peer pressure. If I were to share another physically painful experience from age twelve, one would learn that I "walked off" the pain and might have cursed emotionally as a tough way of verbalizing the pain. As a fifteen-year-old, I might have played it in a stoic silent manner, but with obvious facial expressions letting others know I am hurt but I am handling it. As a twenty-one-year-old, I might let others express my emotions for me, trying to keep calm and cool until receiving the help I need. The concept worth examining here is that behaviors can change when social pressures exist. The pressure to affiliate and assimilate is common and not unique to any specific age group, gender, or culture. The desire to have social affiliation is a way of feeling acceptance from others. Sometimes the ways of the group encourage and alter thoughts, feelings, and behaviors—that do not match well with a person's inner identity—which were consistently shown for several years until becoming shaped into something different than who the individual was/is.

Self Changes: Planned or Unplanned?

At some point in our lives we must intentionally decide when it is emotionally safe and comfortable to share what is really felt internally, rather than behave only in ways that appear socially acceptable. We might recognize certain instances in our lives when we have consciously or subconsciously withheld thoughts, feelings, or actions due to their appearing too different, odd, or unique when compared to others. Under such circumstances, our communication might not merge well with the dominant group's ideas or belief system. The result might be a tendency for us to withhold our expression as a form of self-protection and to avoid a negative backlash from group members.

Another aspect impeding a person's honest self-expression relates to disapproving and unfriendly responses expressed by others. An individual's personal choice of self-expression with different ideas might stimulate unfavorable reactions. These reactions from the group might be communicated in ways that place the real or honest individual at risk for getting hurt through criticism, humiliation, and/or rejection. But when sincere ideas and self-expressions are shared openly, the person has made a decision to be free from the negative effects of social judgments and accept their true inner Core Self.

Understanding oneself is an important part of self-acceptance. The absence of self-understanding may leave a person feeling insecure and unhappy. This is because the person does not clearly recognize their internal Core Self that already exists. Without this knowledge, emotional experiences and outward expression may seem random and will not always feel congruent with the Self.

Temperament, which is part of the Core Self, ultimately relates to thoughts and feelings that are experienced within us and are communicated to others. Knowing the Self should also naturally lead to openness and an embracing of others. Trying to understand and accept another individual is a healthy approach to life, thus creating an opportunity for mutual acceptance with an appreciation of the differences between each other.

We are not always fully aware of what our Core Self actually is, and other parts of our personality are ever changing due to life experiences, education, and other outside influences. Thinking with an open mind allows for personal growth and better self-understanding. Such flexible thinking supplies us with new experiences and opportunities for introspection and personal insight. These moments of self-awareness open us up to further examine the deeper parts of ourselves. It is our core being that exists beyond the social influences in our life. It is more about the essence of what makes us who we are as unique individuals.

Aspects of Individuality

A person's uniqueness can be seen from infancy. Research shows that personality traits appearing early in one's life can be identified later for the same person during adulthood. Our environment contributes to our personality development and cannot be discounted, since it is a significant part of our growth. However, our innate traits along with a temperament style are unique aspects of personality development that are acknowledged in this model. Traits and temperament do merge with life experiences to partially create a distinctive personality. Since each of us is born with a unique combination of genetics, and we all have different personal life histories and social experiences, no two humans will ever be the same.

As young children, we are initially low in or free from inhibitions. What we feel is what we feel. As time progresses, we learn that many of our inner thoughts and emotions do not fit well into what others expect of us socially. The rules that make up societal norms begin to shape our beings and can ultimately dictate a new form of self—but not our true inner self.

It is reasonable to observe and accept social norms while still maintaining individuality. Self-acceptance for how we think and feel should remain important, however there is value in learning general appropriateness within various social situations. As children grow, it is important that they develop the necessary social skills to navigate appropriately within society. It is good to engage others within the boundaries of societal norms. It is also good to maintain personal values and not abandon the parts of the self that seem separate from a group outlook. We can be honest with ourselves about who we truly are and still integrate into society.

As we socially engage our environment, changes to the self begin to emerge. Parts of our personality may get shaped or edited by such things as parental values, educational systems, and social mores. Young children, who were comfortable with genuine emotions and natural reactions to life circumstances, may become self-conscious. Anticipation over others' expectations may prevent the expression of deeper, untampered emotions that we internally feel.

If we choose to be the person we actually are, we could risk ridicule and ostracization from others. However, if we consciously choose to be who we are, then we are actually trusting and believing in ourselves. With this, we can embrace a deeper understanding of who we are. This requires conscious effort and a willingness to experience uninhibited self-acceptance. The choice for self-awareness can be explored any time in a person's life. Through self-awareness, an individual may develop better self-confidence with increased comfort to share and be open. For young people, self-understanding with self-acceptance may help them navigate through life problems and social issues with a greater sense of empowerment.

This model was developed as a means of gaining self-understanding along with the encouragement for us to understand others. The model can be considered both psychological and sociological as it examines the inner self within the context of outside social influences. Looking within the self with self-acceptance is an important component toward self-understanding, since embracing who we are can reduce negative inhibitions and decrease concerns over how we fit within society.

The concept of self-acceptance is familiar in psychology, considering that it is a basic premise from the Humanistic movement. It also supports free-thinking and individualistic insights through the process of personality development. This model is offered as a guide toward gaining self-insight related to each individual's own life history and coupled with the encouragement of acceptance for the self and others.

Accepting Human Variance: We Are Each Unique

When we are open to different people and new ideas, we are able to engage with countless steps of progress, welcoming us to venture onto life's many paths. Social acceptance of human variability helps develop a person's mental and moral character. Different circumstances and experiences can partially contribute to shaping an individual's life perspective. Such variations may also help guide the individual with life goals over time.

At times we are either drawn to a path that is incongruent with our own nature or life's circumstances place us in situations seemingly beyond our comfortable control. These commonly familiar experiences may pull us away from our Real Self and push us in the direction of a disingenuous self, relating us more to a larger group of individuals with dissimilar ideas or values rather than those individuals that better define who we are. It is at this point that we may encounter feelings of emotional discomfort that may lead to depression and anxiety. Whether we act congruently or not, this partially determines the emotional health of one's self.

Altogether, Core Self Theory is a model predominantly created to improve an understanding of ourselves and each other, as unique individuals. Our Core Self is that deep part of the self that is within us and always present. When we understand our inner selves, we can then interact better within our environment and experience enhanced freedom to be honest and real.

When we are our Core Selves in the presence of others, the feeling of obligation to accept unpleasant social standards set by others is absent. Instead, we want to experience harmony with our own thoughts and feelings, while not imposing them on others. It is what happens when a person is true to themself through honest self-expression. It is an ability to acknowledge that a person's internal reactions are truly theirs, and they have the freedom to express themself genuinely.

Chapter 2

Background of Your Core Self

All of us are unique individuals. The way we think and feel directly impacts our actions and how we relate to others. Simply put, our personality develops out of our life histories and genetic makeup. It encompasses our social interactions and reactions to the world around us, combined with established inherited genetics that relate to temperament and traits.

The integration of these components of the self begins in a person's infancy and sets the stage for personality development. On a deeper level, there is a Core Self that is special to each individual. Accepting who we are as our Core Self—and embracing the same for others—is the mission of the Core Self Theory model. The ultimate goal is freedom to be uniquely oneself, without fears of judgment or criticism.

We have all heard commonly repeated statements that encourage self-acceptance with an overtone of not being concerned with the opinions from others. These statements may be spoken as "be who you are," "don't change," or "you have to be yourself." Though these expressions have positive intent and are encouraging, they are actually stressful and challenging for most individuals.

The struggle to be yourself is loaded with self-questions. Here we might process the issue of being oneself through conscious awareness, thinking about what it really means to be real in the presence of others. This, however, can feel risky, with exposure to judgments and criticism. In another approach, we may reactively avoid addressing the challenge of this openness by responding to this concept subconsciously and editing our self to minimize negative repercussions for honesty. Even with a relatively high level of self-acceptance, there is the challenge of feeling social acceptance, something that matters to many of us.

Social Pressures to Join a Group's Mindset

Disapproval through outside judgment can feel harsh and hurtful. Criticism experienced from a fault-finding audience may be expressed directly or indirectly, whether it is communicated by an individual or group of people. Direct criticism can be presented through open verbal statements and taunts. A less direct approach may also get communicated, such as nonverbally through facial expressions or attitudes. Indirect criticism is more ambiguous and may be shared through stated generalizations that come across as unclear or nonspecific. With these types of communications, the person experiences criticism that is negatively implied rather than expressed.

Under such circumstances, the receiver of these exchanges often feels some level of distress. This type of unhealthy criticism may have a result of negatively affecting another's self-esteem. It can also pressure the receiver of the message to change thoughts, feelings, and behaviors to match those of others. This is shaping, and it can prevent movement toward being oneself.

Constructive criticism can be hurtful or helpful, therefore we must consider the source and assess for ourselves what is useful information. Paradoxically, when a person's stated intention of a negative judgment is deemed constructive criticism, there is still an underlying sense of disapproval. Even when the objective is meant to support and help another, it can nevertheless prompt the idea that change is necessary and that "what I am doing is wrong." This is why encouragement is recommended for assisting an individual to do their best and strive toward success.

Sometimes the supportive yet critical approach is productive, especially when presented with honesty and respect. In these circumstances the receiver of such criticism may acknowledge and value the comment(s), since they are genuinely intended to assist them. Such an exchange promotes a willingness to learn and pursue new ideas or edit certain aspects of a presentation. When the communication is presented through genuine and positive intent, it is usually experienced as useful advice meant to be helpful. This form of constructive criticism gets presented through kindness rather than negativity and disapproval.

The goal should never be to change another person. Instead, the intention is to offer honest feedback in reference to another person's approaches, decisions, or actions within a given situation. When thoughts and recommendations are offered with actual care, the receiver will experience respect and understanding, which might stimulate alternative approaches to a given situation.

Acceptance of another person's Core Self is an acceptance of their individuality. The ideal of mutual self-acceptance among people removes the inequity created from criticism and judgment. Integrated parts of the Self exist and create a person's distinctive personality. It develops over time and includes our genetically based temperament and traits as well as our learned behaviors that are influenced by negative and positive life experiences. The remaining component included in this consolidation of self-elements is somewhat theoretical and abstract. It is something that is hard to define, yet separates us from one another. It is that deep core of our inner being that makes us unique individuals.

So, Who Am I?

Throughout history we have sought to understand and describe our inner nature. This quest has been examined philosophically, religiously, and more recently, psychologically. While there are several perspectives regarding our human existence in relation to personality development and motivation, certain aspects of what it means to be human may vary when differentiated among the countless views. Some differences seem subtle, while others are distinctly unalike when comparing and contrasting schools of thought. Certain elements of this knowledge of the self may be either closely aligned or resonate as deficient among scholars. This may depend on a person's background or theoretical orientation.

There are others who wish to simply understand themselves. They carry a valued interest in understanding the self and others with a basic goal of living a happy life. Core Self Theory presents with a perspective that considers the whole person. It supports the view that within ourselves lies a Core Self that proceeds through the progression of our life. Our true being contains an internal presence of a temperament along with a deeper internal psyche, which account for how we manage outside influences and stressors and ultimately affect personality.

Core Self Theory shares related components with the humanistic approach in psychology. Both promote self-acceptance, a movement toward discovering an individual's full potential and celebrating uniqueness. These features are meant to be experienced by everyone. You are encouraged to be free to be who you are just as much as I am encouraged to be me. With such mutual social interest comes the development toward a betterment of society and the promotion of personal improvement for all.

Core Self Theory highlights the need to feel personal self-worth while recognizing the value of other people. It is meant as an optimistic model supporting the elimination of negative judgments for the Self and of others. It encourages self-acceptance through being one's Real or Honest Self with the integration of self-elements to become the whole person.

When understanding a person as a whole being, we should be aware that one carries several separate definable elements within the Self. Each element is important when describing the whole person, but these elements alone do not fully explain the individual. Essentially, the combined qualities of each self-element create a totally original entity that by itself is unique. This similar concept was initially discussed by the Greek philosopher Aristotle (384–322 BC) who wrote about how several things have various elements but do not culminate as simply an aggregate that equals the whole. The sum of the parts when compared to the whole is not the same. The whole may not be considered as simply just less or more but ultimately a separate, distinct entity.

A complication exists when people are reduced to stereotypes, idiosyncrasies, and unique or special qualities that seem to supersede the totality of an individual's complete Self. At times it is as if a single part defines the whole, which is an unnecessary and unfortunate mistake we may fall into. When this occurs, an individual may be given unrealistic praise or undue ridicule, placing them in an unfair position that takes away from the person's true essence.

The Core Self of a person is ever present and contains certain characteristics that help define the individual. The different aspects of the Self are melded together with an individual outcome that may not be replicated by another. This deepest element is the whole Self that combines with our temperament and overall traits along with spiritual and psychosocial experiences.

Appreciating the Self

It is rewarding for an individual to have self-acceptance relating to the positive facets of the Self. This may be achieved through introspection and an outward understanding of one's environment with its surrounding circumstances. It can be a struggle to experience and accept positive aspects of the Self when a mostly unfavorable self-view may become reinforced by important others in a person's life. This is why encouragement, rather than discouragement, is the best option for raising a child. It is also important to offer this type of support to adolescents, especially at home but also in the school setting, sports teams, and other extracurricular activities.

This is additionally true for adults, whether encouragement is given in their work environment or a social organization. Though this sounds familiar, as in positive reinforcement, the act of encouragement sends a constructive message that says, "You are OK" and "I support you." With this type of inspirational motivation, a feeling of safety exists that can build a person's confidence and may cultivate a movement toward self-acceptance as our Core Self. Owning an inner good nature, without guardedness or resistance, promotes positive social interactions and ideally a supportive community.

Humanistic psychologist Abraham Maslow (1908–1970) termed a person's ultimate level of self-acceptance and internal security as Self-Actualization. Through his Hierarchy of Needs, a person may achieve Self-Actualization after first experiencing or embracing the following levels of need fulfillment: physiological needs, safety and security, love and belonging, and self-esteem. Self-Actualization as a developmental achievement means the person has a high degree of self-acceptance and recognizes their personal skills, qualities, and capabilities.

When a person is Self-Actualized they may express themself freely with spontaneity and strive to maximize their inner potential. In comparison to Core Self Theory, such a person behaves as their Real or Honest Self since they are comfortable accepting themself and others. According to Maslow, those who are Self-Actualized value others and carry social interest with a close connection to humanity.

Mutually Caring About Social Interest

The idea that individuals possess social interest was first introduced by Austrian psychiatrist Alfred Adler (1870–1937) in his theory of Individual Psychology. He recognized how people are socially connected through feelings of belongingness within their community. His model views people experiencing social interest through cooperative behavior, which includes a mutual goal of interconnectedness with social interest and the common good for all.

To fully understand the individual, Adler viewed social interest as a pertinent component of the self that is a relevant element helping to develop an individual. The understanding of an individual can be best appreciated by recognizing how social interest intertwines with a person's full environment. This encompasses personal life histories along with social interactions with people involved in the person's life. An individual's movement toward personality development may be understood as a reaction to nature and nurture influences that consolidate with Core Self elements when becoming whole.

A Humanistic Perspective

A person's Core Self may be further understood through the idea of holism. Holism is a concept that focuses on understanding a person as their whole self rather than through a reductionist view, aiming to break down the parts of the self to their most basic elements. Through Core Self Theory, an individual is defined as their own distinct and authentic Self, influenced by several interactive factors. They are not simply explained by a single component, such as genetics or social influences.

The Core Self is composed of elements that are closely interconnected as the whole. Though these parts exist independently, they are also merged together. The elements of the Self are separate by themselves but ultimately emerge as something unique. With holism, the whole is considered greater than the sum of its parts. This view has similarities to Aristotle's belief that the parts make the whole person, not in terms of being greater or lesser but, instead, different. Both consider the whole person as a distinct entity. Core Self Theory views the various elements of the Self as being linked together, which ultimately produces someone unique, special, and distinctive.

Humanistic psychology maintains a perspective close to holism, with an interest in exploring the whole person and recognizing what it is that makes a person unique. This encompasses such things as the emotional, physical, social, and spiritual elements of the self. As a mostly humanistic and positive approach to understanding human nature, Core Self Theory also considers the relationship of the Self's elements linked together to create the individual.

Other important values highlighted in the humanistic model relate to the importance of free will and the appreciation of others through social interest. Such factors lead to self-discovery and to maximizing a person's full life potential so they may experience greater self-acceptance. Similarly, Core

Self Theory conveys the importance of embracing others by supporting an expression of their Honest Self. Who they truly are is of equal significance to who we are as individuals.

Discovering the Different Layers of Myself

We should ultimately try to recognize our genuine internal thoughts as well as our emotional reactions to other people and life situations. What matters is that we try to know what our thoughts and feelings actually are and that we do not try to actively deny them. The choice to think independently and to express real emotions is only part of the process of self-understanding.

We are always free to withhold our personal thoughts and feelings because it is our right to choose what we disclose. This holding back might depend upon a person's surroundings or company at a given time. In some circumstances, choosing to withhold—while not denying what is actually experienced internally—may be emotionally safer.

On the contrary, we may feel totally free to express ourselves honestly. This could be determined by personal needs or purposeful goals that motivate us to share. My feelings are what is real. Having the choice to express these feelings authentically can be cathartic and freeing, as well as strengthening an internal self-value. At this point, a person may feel so comfortably free that they will embrace the parts of the Self that make them whole. These include accepting genuine feelings and consciously understanding that what one feels is real.

Practicing being mindful of our true internal experience may open us up to having better self-acceptance. However, we may not always feel gratified by the responses of individuals or groups who challenge our real internal feelings. Though our awareness is honest, when it is expressed it may be accompanied by feelings of hurt due to social rejection or frustrations felt when receiving negative responses from others.

Acknowledging our true thoughts and feelings may not change the outcome of an uncomfortable situation, but owning our thoughts and feelings may be a first step toward self-acceptance. Whether we share thoughts and feelings openly with others is a choice that ultimately depends on the situation. Our ability to comfortably move forward with others will depend on our own comfort level as well as our social needs. Utilizing a support system for comfort and other outside acceptance may aid to manage potentially hurtful feelings.

Environmental Factors

Our early surroundings, contacts, and personal observations are all part of the Self that contributes to creating the whole personality. Life histories start with the simple basics of one's early environment and what one's life experiences entail as they move forward. A person's cultural background certainly plays a role in defining personality development as well as other life experiences that can include positive as well as traumatic events or how a person was raised by their parent(s). On the side of one's genetics, we can recognize how a specific temperament type and general traits are uniquely part of the Self. Some temperaments and traits are more apparent when a person reaches adulthood, and they remain a fundamental piece of an individual's sense of Self.

With Core Self Theory, a deep understanding of the Self is valued since it includes explaining the internal nature or essence of our being. This profound part of ourselves is our quiddity, that which makes us human and unlike any other living thing. It is our inherent human nature. However, our individual internal being is more specific. It is an intense and higher level of depth unique to each individual that is included in the complete interpretation and appreciation of the whole person or Core Self.

Traits

Other significant parts of personality are our inherent traits. Traits are abundant and represent our basic human presentation, regardless of their high frequency or if they merely appear as idiosyncratic characteristics. Undeniably, specific traits are commonly observed within certain cultural groups and societies. Though often genetically based, they are also likely established through systemic needs or long lived traditions. Sometimes they may exist out of necessity. In other instances they are reinforced as a form of social expectation.

Traits may be present over long periods of time and may be passed on from generation to generation. Such traits can be behavioral, such as being loud and boisterous versus being quiet and meek. Other traits may relate to attitude, such as high levels of confidence compared to timidness. Traits can also be seen physically, as with a person's eye and hair color, or can be movement oriented, such as with facial expressions or manner of walking. These genetic and acquired traits may be considered common within certain communities and also appear to run in families.

In general, traits can be viewed as essential components of a personality, helping define a person's sense of Self. Traits, whether genetically present or influenced by the environment, represent things we can appreciate about ourselves as they contribute to the choices we make. The manner in which we think and feel drives the actions connected to our traits. We all have our own blend of traits that are managed through the unique styles blossoming from our temperament approaches. Temperaments are neither good nor bad. Each of us approaches society and our physical environment with a uniqueness that is personal to us and unlike the special qualities of another.

Temperament

On a deeper level, a person's temperament helps define their manner and approach to life. It is a type of attitude that drives personality through connected thoughts and feelings, and influences trait behavior. Since temperament is widely viewed to be mostly genetically based, we carry a particular innate presentation when it comes to handling situations relating to other people and our environment. We often see children operating within their surroundings in ways that come across as established. They are free to express and react to situations in their unique and personal way. This is because a young child is mostly oblivious to the general rules related to social order and the accepted traditions and mores of a particular culture. However, some young children may express themselves and behave cautiously, but this depends on a child's early shaping and learned consequences based on their upbringing and early life experiences.

For the majority of young and innocent children, they tend to express their temperament styles naturally. For instance, when I interact with my two-year-old granddaughter, I see that her ability to engage me within various settings is totally different from my memories of her mother, my daughter. They do share similar traits, like my granddaughter's ability to fully focus on the things she feels are important or entertaining. Her mother definitely had this trait at that age but presented with a different attitude and demeanor.

Sometimes when my two-year-old granddaughter wants something, she engages me with a strong vocal presence. If I do not respond quickly enough to her requests, she actively engages other adults to prompt my attention toward the needs she has at the moment. The temperament seen here relates to being outwardly assertive and not giving up. If she wants something, she will let others know. If she is not understood, it is important enough for her to persist. On the other hand, her mother, who is my daughter, was equally persistent in stating her needs at a similar age, but her temperament was more reserved and methodical. She was open with what she wanted but could remain patient until she was understood. If she cried about it, it was more out of sadness, while my granddaughter might cry more out of frustration or exasperation.

Another example of temperament differences showed when my granddaughter and I sat together to play and color in her coloring book. Initially, she was cooperative with my method of sharing and participating yet she had her own approach to the playful task, and she guided me. She was initially well focused but progressively lost interest. If I were to continue with my approach, she would have moved on to a different activity. Since I followed her approach, we had fun. I recall similar moments with my daughter. She was also well focused, however her temperament was more easygoing. She was open to waiting and seeing if she might enjoy the activity. If she was no longer interested, she would ask to end it.

Their different dispositions help me to recognize that, though they can experience common traits, they exhibit a different behavior in a similar situation. Approaches were different when encountered with similar items. For this reason, it is important for parents to understand their child's perspective and to work with their temperament or approach to life. Rather than trying to get a child to see things through the parent's eyes, the parent might focus on understanding their child's own internal experience.

Ultimately, the effects of one's temperament suggest a distinguishing, unique approach to engaging one's environment and life situations. Temperament has a strong effect on human development and personality type through its impact on certain behavioral traits. Reactions, guided by temperament regarding different life situations, emerge from inner impulses and inspirations. While a person's traits may be regulated by temperament, they also appear to be commonly linked with family and community influence from a social-behavioral perspective. With Core Self Theory, temperament is considered a mentality guiding a manner and approach to various life occurrences. Our emotional functioning and thought processes impact our social interactions with the world around us.

Quiddity–Haecceity

While quiddity is our "whatness," haecceity is a person's "thisness." The final component associated with understanding personality development relates to the root of the Core Self. As a whole, our Core Self is partially explained by the parts of the Self that were previously discussed, such as social experiences, traits, and temperament. Each of these elements partially contribute to what makes us who we are. But it should be recognized that a person's haecceity also adds to a comprehensive definition of a person's distinguishing characteristics. Haecceity (hak ˈsēədē), as our inherent nature, may be viewed as the deepest part of the Self, our true essence as a person.

Philosophically, this part of the Core Self can be compared to something spiritual. Plato considered the soul to be a person's deep self that is responsible for how we act. He also viewed the soul as immortal and believed it could be reincarnated through a transmigration of the soul after death (metempsychosis.) Also interesting, and partially aligned with Core Self Theory, is the Aristotelian belief that the soul is linked to our bodies, thus giving us life. It is the link between mind and body. Unlike Plato, Aristotle did not view the soul as part of the afterlife but, rather, the essence of a being. He believed there could not be a soul without a body, and the soul is what makes us alive.

In Core Self Theory, this part of the Core Self is the immaterial part of us that influences our thoughts and feelings yet is a distinct piece of our inner whole self, helping to determine who we are as unique human beings. Our haecceity does not consist of physical matter since it is incorporeal and presents more as a life force.

Different religions and philosophies recognize individual uniqueness in human beings while exploring a deeper understanding of what it means to be an individual. That immaterial part of ourselves, that is fundamentally at the center of who we are, has been termed as the energy that gives life to thoughts, feelings, and behaviors. Sometimes it is regarded as the spirit, with a separate structure from the body. But the soul is more commonly viewed as that part of us that gives life to our bodies and interacts with the material world. Our body and soul integrate the pieces of ourselves as we navigate through life.

Within Christianity the soul is considered an unseen part of ourselves that controls our material body. The soul is the breath of life, and it helps communicate our emotional needs and desires. Though the human body is made of physical matter, similar to plants and other living things, we are different because we also have a spirit. Christians recognize this spiritual component since it is what connects us to God. When we pass, the spirit returns to God. But in the living world, we are given life through the soul. The soul is intangible and immaterial, but it is unique to each human being.

The Latin term for the soul is anima, defined as the air, breath, and wind. It includes the presence of thought processes and emotional expression. Similarly, the Greek word psyche (Psyche was the Goddess of the Soul) relates to the term Life Force. Other names used for Life Force are known as Prana (Sanskrit) or Chi/Qi (Taoism), both translating as breath or air. These and other corresponding terms are present among different cultures and religions, and identify a deeper understanding of what it means to be human. They aim to reveal the presence of an intangible energy or Vital Principle, proposing that there are nonmaterial life processes that are not physically explainable. Vitalism supports the concept that human beings have a soul with natural energy, and the soul exists after death due to a Vital Force or Life Force.

Other conceptualizations of the human soul are supported by several other influential philosophies and religions seeking to understand human nature. As a similar concept, our human quiddity and haecceity of the Core Self can be considered the base of our existence, driving the Self to be what it is. It is pervasive, permeating every aspect of our human lives. It is omnipresent, internally central to the core of the Self, going beyond the role of temperament, traits, and personal life experiences.

If one considers their inner Core Self haecceity as a version of the soul, supporting a person's raw and unexplored temperament, then we can say a truly unique person exists. Temperaments may be guided by this part of the Core Self with a progression of influence that regulates our traits. Each of these elements (haecceity, temperament, traits, and life experiences) should ultimately have an impact on the whole of an individual's unique personality development.

Integrating the Self-Elements

When we understand our inner selves, we can naturally choose healthier interactions within our environment without being limited to the social scenarios that can feel unnatural, since they are created by others. As we accept our Core Self in outside social exchanges, we experience the freedom to be ourselves. This is ultimately being more of the Real or Honest Self, as opposed to what will be later referred to as the Lost or Hidden Self.

A healthy life approach permits empowerment for being who we are, without the hindrance of feeling compelled to accept a group's standards that are not comfortably our own. When we are our Core Self, we are in harmony with thoughts and feelings experienced internally while not placing them onto others. This occurs when we are true to ourselves and behaving with sincere self-expression. It is the capacity to accept that we all carry deeper experiences that are truly ours, along with an acceptance of others' freedom to communicate authentically in their own way.

The intention of illustrating Core Self Theory is to help individuals recognize, appreciate, and accept themselves and others as unique and special human beings. The Core Self is a profound integration of our personality parts that creates an individual who carries a depth that is special and totally unique to each human being. Accepting who we are and embracing the same for others is a meaningful goal that ultimately helps to improve mental health with resultant improvement of social interest.

Chapter 3

Know Thyself

I remember seeing my firstborn daughter as she learned to communicate with me and others. She had a happy disposition. She also had a soft yet assertive side. She smiled when feeling joy. She laughed when surprised or entertained. She cried and pouted when things did not go her way. All these qualities could be observed in this one-year-old child. Her temperament and traits were also apparent in her at an even younger age.

As she got older, she held the same temperament and traits but had also experienced changes in her social environment. Not only did she experience a physical change, such as moving away from the house she knew and loved, but she also lost regular contact with my wife's family, which included grandparents and other family members. The change was not traumatic, but it was still a change. She had to adapt to her new environment along with schedule changes, such as my longer time away from home due to work and her eventual placement in nursery school.

Added to her environmental changes, she transitioned from an only child status to an older sister status, with the addition of both a younger sister and brother to play with and lead. It was entertaining to see her orchestrate play activity that clearly maintained her leadership role, while also seeing her full range of emotions revealed when playing was fun and lively or when things did not work out as she planned. I recall her putting a play together, as she often did, and struggling to get the cooperation of her brother. Her younger sister did her best to keep true to the role assigned in the play, but the frustrations the eldest felt were familiar to those she expressed in other similar situations. To this day, similar dynamics can be seen when she and her siblings try to work together on some collaborative project.

The little one-year-old child can still be seen in my adult daughter. Though more sophisticated in her approach, her similar attitude and emotional reactions get communicated when she engages with her siblings just as they have consistently been since their own early youth. I have always known my children's Core Self. It is the deeper part of themselves that goes beyond simply traits or learned behaviors. Even when they might become affected by outside influences, I believe I know what they are truly thinking and feeling since I have watched them grow and maintain certain qualities that uniquely define them.

Encouraging the Core Self of Children

Observing the actions of our young children can feel good. We see them as sincere and honest little beings with uninhibited behaviors. When our toddlers are free to express themselves naturally and without fears of judgment, they are revealing their core being, their Core Self. Such children behave with complete openness and appear oblivious to critical thoughts and reactions from the people around them. Under the healthiest circumstances, the majority of their behaviors should receive support and encouragement by the people in their life.

Supportive parenting is an ideal. This approach is best, even when a child is too young to speak or understand language. There are several forms of communication, outside of words, that convey supportive emotional information and can be understood by a child through consistent presentations of this caring approach. A parent's oral volume and intonation, their eye contact with encouraging facial expressions, or a gentle touch or pat on the back are other forms of communication that may be felt and understood by young children. I often observe such actions as I watch my daughter interact with her newborn child. Sometimes the baby makes direct eye contact and smiles at her mother. With this, my daughter reacts by saying a few sweet words while caressing her daughter's face and ending with a gentle kiss on her forehead. This should be viewed as a genuine support of the child's good-natured temperament and not simply as behaviors that are reinforced by both mother and child. The child is encouraged to express the feelings she exudes naturally.

Encouragement from other people in a child's life is like a green light telling them to proceed and move forward with who they are. When we experience such support, it feels validating and prompts the furtherance of more expression and action. It helps the internal become external. On the contrary, when we experience discouragement from others while being authentic, we feel various levels of embarrassment, wrongfulness, or shame. Somehow we believe we are not entitled to be who we are. This is either conveyed through direct or indirect communication. Whether negative shaping is made obvious or passed on in the form of subtleness, the message is still felt as something that is wrong or not suitable to share.

I am reminded of certain family friends who took the time to provide support for their children's interests. Not only did they produce outlets for their children to express themselves uniquely, they also took their opinions and ideas seriously. If one son showed an interest in baseball, they were supportive and placed him on a team. If the interest changed, the parents would encourage their son to explore other interests. When their child shared values or opinions, there was guidance and problem-solving offered by the parents. The children grew up with high levels of confidence due to support; as adults, these same children showed freedom to try new things and expressed themselves uninhibitedly. This relates to the parents' encouragement approach that allows Core Self strengths to emerge, even when expressions of choices were not mainstream.

While life experiences partially explain an individual's style of life and how they present to others, it is merely one element related to personality development. Shaping also has its place in understanding how and why people act the way they do. Encouragement and discouragement of what might be considered positive and negative behaviors will become reinforced.

We are influenced by things that are given or taken away, such as with rewards and punishments. As a means of trying to get our needs met, we may become susceptible to criticism or praise. This influence may be communicated by parents, other family members, teachers, and a peer social system. It may actually change our direction from what was initially honest and sincere behavior to what now becomes contrived and readjusted.

We could lose our faithfulness to our Core Self due to unintended shaping responses. When this occurs, there may be a general sense of emotional discomfort. Genuine, unlearned communications may elicit unexpected negative consequences, thus making it more comfortable and secure to choose "getting along" instead of showcasing a unique identity that results in a person's feeling like an outcast. Life experiences and social shaping certainly do impact personality development, but they do not account for the deeper aspects of the Self that are internal and most natural.

A child's start of school is an example of social discomfort. The child may have little socializing experience. In fact, they may believe that their behaviors and emotional responses are socially acceptable to others within various interactive situations. What is eventually discovered is that their school has rules that must be followed, and peer groups determine what is socially appropriate. Even when there may be different communication rules at home, there may be shaping in the school setting that teaches the child what behaviors are rewarded or penalized. One's Core Self may not have the acceptance in their new environment as it did in a safer environment such as at home.

As parents we often see our children struggling with a Core Self presentation while simultaneously trying to get along with outside social demands. This is a natural part of emotional growth and communication development. While it is important that parents stay aware of their child's struggles, they can offer support as well as guidance through helping with social skills, personal boundaries, and important values. Parental guidance certainly depends on the child's individual uniqueness along with the social circumstance presented. Parents will be most helpful by recognizing their children's Core Self thoughts and feelings, and helping them explore options for handling difficult social situations.

Parts of the Self Interacting Throughout Life Development

Temperament and trait research have sought to understand additional factors involved in creating an individual's personality. It is recognized that traits observed in young children can continue for the entirety of that person's life. Each of us has some special combination of traits with high and low levels of intensity that contribute to our personality formation. Some obvious traits run in families, while other traits are less noticeable and seem individualized. Additional traits coupled with some other idiosyncratic characteristics may create a strength for someone or, in other instances, a limitation. Our traits impact our personal thoughts and reactions to external stimuli, which are separate and distinctive from how others would react to the same stimuli. We are all unique individuals.

Some children may appear anxious and easily frustrated, while others present as mellow and able to go with the flow. Some children are naturally expressive, open, and free to verbalize their feelings, yet other children are the opposite, as they present as shy, emotionally withholding, and nonverbal regarding what they are experiencing internally. There are endless trait variations that contribute to an individual's personality. Our differences exist with a vast array of trait combinations. Every child possesses two unique family branches from which they genetically receive traits from both biological parents' families. Even within the same family of the same biological parents, no two children are completely alike, not even with twins.

In fraternal twin studies, we recognize that genetic traits are similarly present the same as they are for regular siblings of the same parents. Identical twins may initially carry the same DNA from their parents, but they do not always develop in exactly the same way. Changes may occur after the two embryos form, thus creating differences. Further, environmental factors eventually play a significant role in a person's growth.

Life experiences partially explain variations in personalities. In addition, the development of certain emotional problems or psychiatric disorders will occur approximately 50 percent of the time for identical twins who were separated at birth. They should carry close to exact genetics but encounter different environmental experiences. One twin may later receive a particular diagnosis while the other twin does not. While this is noteworthy, it is clear that genetics alone do not completely account for a person's temperament, traits, and ultimately their personality. Instead, it helps us understand the importance of our biological makeup when addressing the question of nature versus nurture. Environmental factors, such as life experiences and cultural backgrounds, carry an impact on personality development and interact with a person's general temperament.

From childhood through early adulthood, we experience developmental challenges that occur during the process of our personality formation. Life experiences, along with various assumed family and social roles, ultimately consolidate and combine with biological effects to partially define us as individuals. As we are developing physically, emotionally, and intellectually, certain parts of our Core Self remain steady and appear to exist over time. Temperament, as a part of the Core Self, exists as early as infancy and remains a basic component of a person's personality.

In some instances temperament may appear to adjust to our developmental stages, especially as we grow older. Such an example would be the emotional pain we experience when we become hurt or sad about something. As a child we might act out or cry; as a young adult we may express feelings verbally and utilize feedback when appropriate. At these different developmental stages, the internal feeling of hurt and sadness is probably similar, but the reaction is conveyed in another way. The same Core Self is present at all life stages but is expressed differently.

Even when there are several life-changing experiences and diverse social encounters, there is a natural internal disposition that remains constant and unchanged, even if it is repressed. Perhaps subconscious defenses hamper thoughts and feelings that are too raw or uncomfortable to express, placing a person in a place of vulnerability. True expression and a revealing of one's traits may be squelched in order to get along with others or even gain acceptance from individuals or groups.

Challenges in Knowing Oneself

Personality formation develops as a process of inner growth and eventual individuation. This is a particularly stressful time. Emotional experiences during one's youth—from constant pressure to assimilate within peer groups—can often challenge a child's own uniqueness. Though there may be an internal desire for social acceptance during one's early life and adolescence, this can also be felt in adulthood and often continues throughout a person's lifespan.

Children will try minimizing group rejections and avoiding feelings of exclusion, even though they might have their own independent thoughts or personal opinions that are contrary to the popular design of how things are expected to be experienced. Personal individual traits, different from a dominant group, can increase the likelihood of negative reactions by group members due to one's own individuality. Children encounter peer judgments through rejection or disapproval, often through superficial issues related to a person's outward presentation with such things as hairstyle, clothing choice, weight, or physical awkwardness. However, each child is a unique and distinct individual that has an inner Core Self wanting social connection and acceptance.

Personality traits, in the context of Core Self Theory, are viewed as persistent and continual patterns of behavior that can be influenced by our thoughts and emotions. More than that, temperament can impact trait intensity and the portrayal of our trait behaviors. As previously mentioned, traits are generally consistent over time. For example, if a person acts positive and is verbal and extroverted among a group of strangers, we would expect similar trait behaviors to get repeated into the future and at different functions. Though circumstances and surroundings may change slightly, a person guided by their traits will not likely change. Also, they will behave similarly in different settings because traits, influenced by thoughts and emotions, are generally stable over time.

Similar traits among different individuals often present as indistinguishable on the surface. However, with deeper analysis it is observable that they are qualitatively separate as independent variations to commonly known traits. Each person with the trait will exhibit a unique presentation that corresponds to their own inner temperament. These individuals all differ yet carry the same general traits. For instance, honesty as a trait has different variations depending on the person exhibiting the trait. If the trait is influenced by a person with an anxious type of temperament, we may see honesty depicted as a type of forced sharing with underlying fears of punishment. Alternatively, if honesty is guided by someone with a conscientiously minded temperament, honesty may present as a positive ideal with strong moral grounds.

Our Temperament Influencing Our Traits

Models representing personality trait theories often use the terms "trait" and "temperament" interchangeably. For the sake of clarity, a delineation and description of these words seems necessary. Within the Core Self Theory model, traits and temperament are different categories yet work together toward defining personality. As discussed, traits represent different characteristics of an individual that partially set the foundation of a personality in development. A trait is essentially a type of descriptor identifying the activity or style for someone that is recognizable and relatable to most of us.

The trait itself does not determine the presentation of behavior since a trait may be influenced by other psychosocial factors and the temperament we have possessed from early in our lives. American psychologist Gordon Allport, who was an early developer of Trait Theory, actually went through an English language dictionary and identified over 4,000 words that describe various personality traits. His model went further and organized traits or personality characteristics into three different categories. He referred to them as either Cardinal traits, Central traits, or Secondary traits.

Among these differing trait levels, Cardinal traits are most rare and can represent a person's dominant characteristic. In part, these traits tend to appear later in life and can describe a person as ultimately the trait itself, such as being highly social, benevolent, artistic, or even evil. The trait can often relate to a person's passion or interest. A Cardinal trait is something a person is generally known for or is a quality they appear to represent. Examples of this include Mother Teresa, who was known to be the epitome of goodness, while someone like Albert Einstein is identified as intelligent.

Less profound but most common are the Central traits. They can be viewed as general characteristics existing within all of us. These traits impact our behavior and help describe our personality. Traits we use to describe ourselves and others fall into this category. For example, honesty, mellowness, dependability, and loyalty are all traits that we possess and might demonstrate at varying degrees. We might also show these traits at different times in our lives. They are general attributes that can form the basic components of our personality.

The final trait type in Allport's categorical hierarchy is the Secondary trait. These are not as obvious as Central traits. They are characteristics that are usually displayed in only certain conditions or circumstances, such as with anxiety, frustration, or discomfort. The trait might emerge, but it depends on the specific situation. Though most of the time we may represent ourselves consistently with a fixed set of traits, there are certain moments when other traits emerge and get revealed. Such traits may be seen under times of stress or appear as a reaction to a particular person or situation. One's general temperament type certainly has an influence over how the self is internally experienced, and it is a significant factor relating to trait expression.

In Core Self Theory, temperament refers to the way one handles their traits. Temperament is an underlying mood and mode influencing how traits are managed. A basic premise of Core Self Theory is that temperament is biologically influenced. A child is born with unique genetics and neurochemistry, creating a certain temperament type. It is innate and not a learned emotion or behavior.

Ultimately, a temperament presents as a pattern of expressiveness that partially affects the way we engage our environment. Our temperament influences our behavioral traits. When we say someone is behaving "temperamentally," we are describing an emotional state that corresponds to that person's internal "nature." The way a person reacts to various circumstances comes from within and is expressed through traits they carry. Some of our traits appear genetically linked and are in common with particular family members, but one's temperament determines more of their unique manner and approach to different happenings. It is essentially the emotional functioning of how we behaviorally react to the world around us.

Learning and Accepting the Unique Individuality of Children

As parents, many of us share the common belief that it is most appropriate to strive in being fair by treating all of our children equally. It is often described as the ideal way to raise our youth, which is hard to argue. The reality is that this method, though defined as a model approach, is not usually followed. We may commonly hear children describe how things actually are, such as how "unfair it is that an older sibling got to stay up late, yet they never got to have that privilege" or questions like "why can't I walk to the store on my own since my brother was allowed to do it?" The simple reason is that these are different children with separate temperaments and varied traits.

In some situations we might support a particular activity of a certain child, but it may not always be appropriate for others at the same age. This is not to say that general rules, morals, and values should not be taught and reinforced equally within the family framework, because such consistency can contribute to the structuring of a healthy democratic family system. But in practicality, it is better to acknowledge that each child is unique and can benefit from separate, personalized parenting approaches.

For instance, most children within a family are raised with common values. Perhaps one value is to "be kind to others." While one child is kind but discriminates between those who appear safe and those who may be potentially dangerous, another sibling might be completely open and free among all people and at all levels without differentiating. The first child may need less monitoring and be permitted to have more social freedom than the second child, due to their different interpretations of the value. This is likely related to the child's temperament, past experiences, or level of intelligence. Whichever the case, not all children should have equal rules when they all have different needs.

Expectations may exist when teaching or positively guiding our children to behave in certain ways. We may want them to follow our directives and hope they will choose or naturally follow what is being taught. With certain children, we may want to reconsider our expectations if the child struggles to understand. In such situations a parent will benefit by viewing the world through the child's uniqueness. When a parent's temperament is different from their child's, a parent can become consciously aware of this and purposely choose to match and pace with their child's life approach. This form of accommodation helps the child adapt to changes or directions through better connection and support.

If Johnny is told that he is responsible for cleaning the bathroom, showering, and brushing his teeth before bedtime each evening, the expectation is that these tasks get done without reminders. However, if Johnny is easily distractible and does not fulfill these obligations without prompting, it may not always mean he is resistant or oppositional. Instead, there may be a genuine desire to fulfill expectations, yet he struggles to focus and may require a different intervention. The parent may take this opportunity to teach organizational skills and completion of tasks so that the child who is struggling with the completion of certain tasks has an opportunity to succeed.

A child's future interactions are not solely determined by temperament and traits. They are also influenced by significant people in a child's life. These well-intentioned people may be encouraging and want to guide a child with general behavioral methods. As discussed, this approach is not always ideal because it can miss the understanding of a particular child's unique approach to life. It misses their individuality and positive intention. Parents as well as teachers may better benefit children by learning to modify their own communication styles and teaching approaches to properly adjust to a child's temperament.

Though one's Core Self is unique for an individual, there may be value in surrounding oneself with others who share common traits and temperaments, thus creating a closer fit through mutual understandings. This might create more freedom to reveal the Core Self in the presence of others. Parents can do so by enrolling their children in activities where they share similar interests with others. Activities could vary from physical, spiritual, or social. The child's temperament and distinct approach to life will likely benefit from an appropriate guidance that is a "Goodness of Fit" experience, which should improve harmony between the child's temperament and their environment.

Alexander Thomas and Stella Chess, who researched and developed the Goodness of Fit concept, viewed a child's trait preferences as a result of how their mind functions based on their genetics as well as early psychosocial factors. They saw that infants carry unique interactions with caregivers and the environment as they express their needs. Their action types were also found to continue into later life. Thomas and Chess further recognized that problems exist for children when temperament is not acknowledged or accommodated. In such circumstances, there is a "Poorness of Fit," which increases the probability of social and behavioral struggles when certain traits may not easily fit within a person's environment.

Indeed better strategies are necessary for adults to follow when raising children. The proper aim here is to encourage youths, from their toddler years to their teenage years, to truly be themselves and know they are remarkable human beings who are worth the time and effort to be guided with supportive understanding. We must recognize that a child's temperament influences the way they behave as well as how children manage certain traits when interacting with others. After acknowledging and accepting a person's temperament, we can better understand and appreciate their actions to engage them constructively.

Thomas and Chess considered there to be nine basic behavior traits representing the elements related to temperament types. Behaviors for each of these traits have variation and are on a continuum. The traits are briefly summarized below:

- **Activity Level:** Amount of physical energy, motor activity.
- **Rhythmicity:** Regularity, predictability, and routines with biological functions with such things as eating, waking, and sleeping.
- **Distractibility:** Attention span during an activity, level of focus, and concentration when there are external stimuli.
- **Intensity of Mood Expression:** Level of reaction to a situation regardless of being positive or negative, emotional response level.
- **Sensory Threshold:** Amount of a sensitivity to stimuli such as light, sound, and touch.
- **Approach/Withdrawal:** Response to new and different situations and strangers, eager to connect versus hesitant.
- **Adaptability:** Ability to manage new transitions and changes in the environment, capability of fitting into new situations.
- **Persistence/Attention Span:** Time of focus on a particular task or activity.
- **Quality of Mood:** Overall mood or disposition such as happy or sad, positive or negative, serious or playful, optimistic or pessimistic.

These nine traits are critical to further understand the Thomas and Chess model as it relates specifically to temperament. The temperament types for young children generally fall into one of three categories: Easy, Difficult, and Slow to Warm. There are also some individuals who carry a mixture of these behavioral styles, but most will fall into one of these classifications.

- **Easy:** Generally positive and happy, behaviorally active, able to respond comfortably to new situations, regular biological habits like eating, waking, and sleeping routines, approachable, reacts to stress with low to moderate intensity.

- **Difficult:** May be fussy, cries about new things and adapts slowly, problems adjusting to new situations, may have irregular biological habits and routines (eating, waking, sleeping), withdraws from new situations, struggles to adapt, intense emotional reactions to stress, and communicates negative moods with increased intensity.

- **Slow to Warm:** Appears shy and guarded, may be good natured but may project a negative mood, low activity as a baby, takes time adjusting to new experiences, initially withdraws from new situations but may eventually become more comfortable.

The above traits and temperaments were studied by Thomas and Chess in their famous New York Longitudinal Study conducted from 1956 to 1988. Over that time, they examined and classified traits and temperament types through a sample of 133 infants until adulthood. Up to the age of two, the researchers engaged the parents of these children, presenting them with questionnaires and conducting interviews. They then followed the children until adulthood to explore their social and emotional development. Findings demonstrated consistency for temperament types continuing over time. Easy children, for example, were likely to show better life adjustment compared to Difficult children in their early adulthood. Studies by other theorists and researchers who followed Thomas and Chess support similar findings that there is a tendency to carry certain temperament traits into adulthood.

For instance, an Easy child who is calm, cooperative, generally happy, and responsive to others will likely grow up to be even-tempered, open to collaborating with others, present with a positive demeanor, and be comfortable in social situations. A Difficult child might be seen as fussy, someone who struggles in unfamiliar surroundings, has intense reactions, and has irregular habits. As an adult this person might exhibit similar behaviors by appearing irritable, reclusive, displaying negative emotions, and having inconsistent routines. The Slow to Warm child presents as shy, inactive, and with guarded emotions. In adulthood this person may internally be good-natured but outwardly will appear as negative and disengaged.

Granted, there is some variability for the propensity to be completely consistent with an early temperament type. Changes might be attributed to other aspects of a person's life that are more environmental and relate to their culture, social roles, and personal life experiences. Individual and family developmental stages—and how they are handled—may also influence personality growth as one is maturing. Child-rearing practices, coming from dysfunctional family systems and socioeconomic status, contribute as a role affecting temperament and trait variations. However, through the Thomas and Chess model, it is generally recognized that temperament is primarily established through genetics and is relatively steady into adulthood.

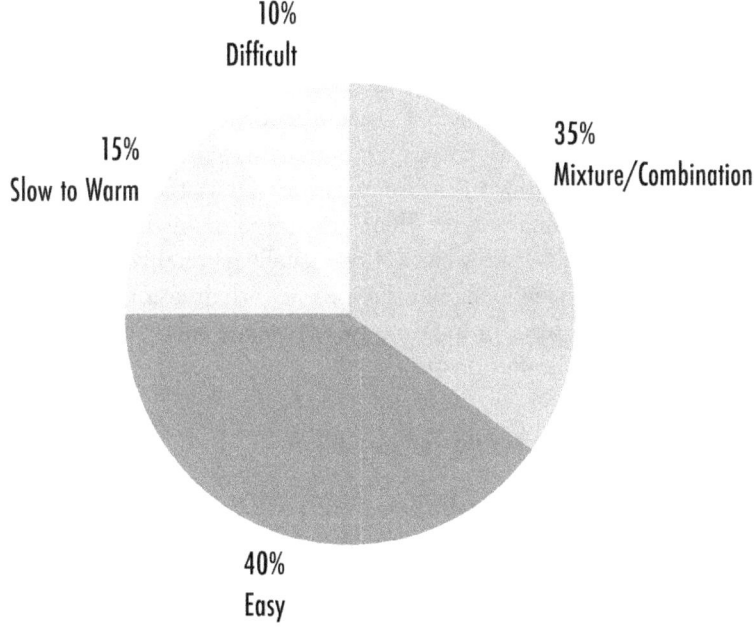

Figure 1. A general breakdown of temperament types as they apply to Thomas and Chess's Temperament Study.

Realize that in Core Self Theory, it is not assumed that individuals can be easily generalized or quantified to fit into an algorithm of certain personality typologies. Although tests for several self-reporting personality inventories are known to be fairly accurate, especially those with high validity and reliability, there are still elements of the Self that are missing. The problem with classifying certain personalities into specific categories is that the uniqueness of the individual is absent. In Core Self Theory, it is recognized that no two individuals are the same, let alone any of the eight billion humans living on this earth possessing the same personality. It is obviously impossible to characterize any two people within a certain personality classification as being exactly the same.

All traits that compose specific personality types have defining qualities of greater or lesser values, thus generating unique differences within specific personality types. For instance, some personality tests use spectrums with two polar ends to show a person's degree of strength for a particular trait. Introversion/Extroversion is commonly used on a spectrum scale with a person landing on one side or the other. Theoretically, on a scale of one (extreme introversion) to one hundred (extreme extroversion), scores of fifty-five or ninety-five will both get recognized as extroversion. Yet the fifty-five score lies closer to an introversion trait score, while the ninety-five score of extroversion is very high. These are traits in common but with very different levels of intensity creating large or micro variations within the personality type. Now imagine score variations for all the traits making up any one specific personality type. There are far too many differences within this personality type, and they cannot be casually generalized for each person. However, if we view personality types with their accompanying traits as truly generalized descriptors, we may appreciate such definitions while understanding their limitations.

Earlier Historical Insights into Temperament

Having approached the discussion of how personality typologies do not fully describe an individual's unique personality, it is also important to address that the individual's underlying temperament, as a basic component of the Core Self, is a valued descriptor helping define who they are and how they operate in their environment. It is helpful for us to understand deeper parts of ourselves and others, as our temperament emerges as a deeper essence of our being.

Temperaments emanate in the form of emotional expressiveness that guide us toward the management of our personal dominant traits. It is hard to precisely define all the distinctive qualities that are included in an individual's temperament, because all temperaments are also unique. But as it was discussed with traits and various personality types, common characteristics may exist representing one's nature with identifying elements making up certain categories.

The original background of studying and defining different temperaments emerged out of the protopsychological theory of the Four Temperaments. This was first introduced by the Greek physician Hippocrates (460 BC–370 BC), who is known as the Father of Medicine. The theory was based on his belief that the four bodily fluids (blood, phlegm, yellow bile, and black bile) impact a person's personality traits, moods, and behaviors. With this theory, temperament is determined by the relative proportions of these humors and may be out of balance through either an excess or deficiency of them. The resulting imbalance was thought to be comparative to one's getting a disease or ailment, as well as generating various behavioral and mood patterns of temperament. Hippocrates also believed that when the body was considered healthy, the four humors would be in balance. This balance was called Eukrasia, meaning normal health and a state of well-being.

Later, Greek physician and philosopher Galen (129 AD–216 AD) added to the four temperament theory by including the humors' interaction with bodily organs and their mechanisms associated with human development. He believed each of these humors have a corresponding temperament with general descriptors, which became known as Sanguine, Phlegmatic, Choleric, and Melancholic. While a person may have one of the four temperaments, it is also possible for a person to hold combinations of them. These mixed types include parts of more than one temperament, which may carry familiar traits from each type. For example, a Sanguine-Choleric temperament may share socializing and extroversion as common traits. In a different example, a Sanguine-Melancholic type might possess an overlap or blend of its two temperament orientations, thus creating variations of their characteristics or inclusion of mixed qualities that could include such traits as empathy, along with optimism and an analytical approach to life stressors.

The four fundamental temperaments are generalized as a means of defining and categorizing individuals' tendencies, however, the uniqueness of the individual is still absent with such broad classifications. What is interesting is that these models of temperaments were developed as a way to describe that deeper foundation of personality development. Starting with Hippocrates and through today's modern personality theorists, there are life observations, research studies, and philosophical debates trying to specify the parts of the self that ultimately define our personality. For now, with the purpose of recognizing how traits can be influenced by a temperament typologies, general examples related to Hippocrates's and Galen's theories are described below as the four temperament types:

- **Sanguine (Blood):** extroverted, energetic, optimistic, enthusiastic, social, adventurous, confident, free with emotions, easygoing. They may also be reckless, impulsive, attention seeking, moody, have poor concentration, and need reassurance.

- **Phlegmatic (Phlegm):** warm, relaxed, giving, peaceful, empathetic, sensitive, responsible, honest, consistent, cooperative, patient, creative, logical, practical, has a stable mood, likes to spend time with small group of friends and is content spending time alone, abides by and enforces rules. They may also be resistant to change, indecisive or neutral, unenthusiastic, judgmental, and have low energy.

- **Choleric (Yellow Bile):** extroverted, social, quick-thinking and feeling, determined, persistent, ambitious, logical, open, direct with people, high energy, self-confident, is a leader. They may also be highly emotional, short tempered, unable to accept criticism, irritable, impulsive, and domineering.

- **Melancholic (Black Bile):** introverted, patient, analytical, detail oriented, wise, sensitive, creative, self-motivated, self-reliant, thoughtful, empathetic, task oriented, efficient, hold high standards. They may also be overthinkers prone to self-reflection, reserved, withdrawn socially, and perfectionistic.

Present day medicine does not define a set connection between the bodily humors and personality development; however, the four temperaments are frequently utilized as the basis of several personality and trait models of today. For instance, the four temperaments have influenced various person-ality tests including the Meyers-Briggs Type Indicator (MBTI) and the Fundamental Interpersonal Relations Orientation-Behavior (FIRO-B). Also, the scientist and behavior theorist Ivan Pavlov derived his own four temperaments, which were identified as Lively (Sanguine), Calm Imper-turbable (Phlegmatic), Strong Excitatory (Choleric), and Weak Inhibitory (Melancholic) temperament types.

Alfred Adler later created the psychological model of Individual Psychology with a theory of personality development through his four Styles of Life concept. It included Socially Useful (Sanguine), Getting or Leaning (Phlegmatic), Ruling and Dominant (Choleric), and Avoiding (Melancholic). According to Adler, a Style of Life appears at an early age, and it is a result of one's unique abilities combined with childhood history and life situations. Similar to Core Self Theory, Adler did not support the notion of personality types as general labels for individuals. This is because when people are viewed as "types," the importance of each individual's uniqueness may be overlooked. Instead, Adler's Individual Psychology identified patterns of behavior that relate to a person's lifestyle that began in early childhood.

How Children Can Benefit from Empathetic Parenting

As was previously mentioned, based on a child's temperament there are important empathetic approaches that can help parents better connect to their children. In general, children can benefit emotionally and intellectually when being raised through the Goodness of Fit model. This should be viewed as a fair and supportive process of interactive guidance. It includes parental understanding with specific direction that matches a child's unique approach to life. Equal levels of this form of parenting should also be experienced among other siblings within a family. Under this model, none of the children would receive preferential treatment. Instead, they would obtain what they need, which might be based on their inner Core Self.

Remember, temperament is merely one component of personality. It relates to how we approach things in life, and it naturally influences a person's traits and decision making. The total personality includes all parts of the Self that impact emotions, thoughts, and behaviors. Insights into the different temperament types may influence our interactions with others and ultimately aid in social harmony through personal openness and acceptance of others.

Supportive parenting with an empathetic understanding of each child's temperament style has advantages that should improve family relations and may decrease conflicts. Expectations for a child to perceive and interpret communications from a parent's perspective may be less important than having a parent understand the child's orientation. This is especially true for a parent and child who have different temperament styles when approaching life situations. The parent can try to view the world through the eyes of the child. This perspective aids with a direction that is more encouraging and productive. With this, the child is more likely to engage in situations productively and try to accomplish certain goals with a positive attitude.

I recall working with an adolescent who was diagnosed with Autism Spectrum Disorder. He was brought into therapy for depressive symptoms, but he also showed limitations with his social skills. He struggled to communicate his thoughts and feelings effectively. When he did try to communicate with peers or adults, it appeared awkward. He did well academically while attending public school. He was receiving academic services through his school to make accommodations for his disability; this helped him succeed. His parents were supportive of their son. They recognized that he had strengths, such as perseverance, as well as a willingness to pursue goals that were important to him. His parents were encouraging and had a desire to help their son transfer to a four-year university after high school. This was what the son wanted. They had concerns that were less about his future academic success and more related to his challenge to make friends and his awkwardness in social situations.

It was helpful that his parents wanted to listen to their son's hopes and desires. They did not impose their own ideas of what they thought he should do. Instead, they did what they had always practiced: They asked their son what he wanted and how they could help to support him. If they had ideas for a direction, they addressed them openly and not as a directive. They understood the importance for their son to feel independent and yet be able to ask for help when needed. This was a good approach, and I could see that trust was high from the son toward his parents.

When our children have ideas, we can listen. As long as we do not foresee significant problems arising from the choices they make, we can be more supportive rather than have critical apprehension. It is also valuable to work with our children through their own temperament or approach to the world. With the case of this client, the parents understood their son's disabilities but maximized his drive to succeed and engage others socially despite his limitations. Acknowledging a child's productive and healthy progress can be experienced as rewarding, and it is likely to be replicated and refined in the future.

Positive and supportive understanding by a parent through a Goodness of Fit approach may be seen in the following examples:

- A Slow to Warm child, as described in the Thomas and Chess model, may also carry traits that are known to represent a Melancholic temperament type under Galen's theory. In this scenario the child is introverted and prefers independent activities rather than their feeling discomfort when engaging in team sports. Though the parent might believe that such physical activity and social interaction are in the child's best interest, it might be more advantageous for the parent to change expectations. The parent could edit the plan by introducing a different, more individualistic type of sport, like swimming or tennis. This might allow the child to experience a sport independently while also having a physical activity that puts them in the company of peers, as well as placing them in socially competitive situations.

- Another example is a child with a Sanguine temperament who also appears to carry a combination of Easy and Difficult temperaments under the Thomas and Chess model. This child likes to have fun, is playful, and is expressive with positive emotions but will also become easily frustrated. The child also struggles to follow structure and has problems finishing basic chores, as demonstrated by incompletion of household tasks. While the parent might define the child's behavior as resistant and uncooperative, they can instead choose to encourage task completion by breaking down large tasks into smaller ones and using praise as a means of positive reinforcement. This might be a better Goodness of Fit when considering the child's temperament type.

With both examples, the parent is demonstrating an understanding of their child's temperament style while still providing necessary guidance and requiring cooperation from the child. In other situations, the parent may have a similar temperament to their child's. This would most likely make parenting and understanding the child a little easier. However, when temperaments are different, the parent is challenged to tune into their child's internal and external experience of the world. Being aware of differences improves communication and enables better cooperative skills. Adjusting expectations and creating better directive approaches should make parenting less complicated for more positive end results.

Teachers Connecting with Students

Empathy as a form of guidance is also useful in the school setting. Teachers can help engage students through this same kind of open-minded parenting approach, when necessary. Though all peers should still receive equal, comparable levels of supportive guidance, a student with more specific needs might benefit from a teacher's compassionate consideration through a Goodness of Fit type model.

Creative approaches that better match the child's temperament style should increase the likelihood of improving motivation and understanding. The goal is to determine how to best relate to a child while promoting learning, whether in academics or in improving social skills with better peer interactions. A positive outcome ultimately results in helping children engage with peers through cooperative learning skills that are developed within a supportive peer environment.

There are students who struggle to blend in with their peers due to poor social skills. Sometimes their temperament presents as standoffish, detached, or withdrawn when they do not know how to "fit in." Peers may avoid engaging with these students because they do not understand their temperament style and label the student as "weird" or "awkward." In such situations, peers may act rejectingly, causing the student to become more solitary. Here, the student may miss opportunities to engage with others, since they are not welcomed by their peer group.

A teacher can identify a student's struggles through simple observation. Their follow-up could involve helping the student engage with their peers by using a different skill set. Perhaps the teacher can publicly recognize unique strengths belonging to the student. This can serve as a self-esteem boost for the isolated student, while also modeling positive social engagement in front of their peers.

For example, the student might have a clever sense of humor or possess a certain knowledge from a personal hobby or books read on a particular subject of interest. One or more of the student's strengths may be highlighted, which often increases a curiosity and further interest from peers. Here, the teacher helps the misunderstood student by accentuating parts of their Self that are now noticeable and valued. A certain worth may now be seen in a skill set that was previously unappreciated.

Educators may have unique opportunities to rearrange obstacles and options for students as well as help direct them toward alternative possibilities for achieving successes. They can orchestrate the variables, which may mean they must view a student's struggles through the student's eyes. They may find simple modifying adjustments that enhance the child's educational experience and lead to improvements in learning and raise self-esteem. Special Education teachers and school psychologists may also try to incorporate student accommodations when appropriate. For instance, a student with focusing problems and poor attention span might benefit when seated in the front of the classroom instead of the back or middle sections. Another example is a child who experiences greater stability and comfort from quiet surroundings for test taking. Such a change of setting decreases unnecessary interruptions and allows for better focus rather than feeding into outside distractions.

Some children diagnosed with Attention Deficit/Hyperactivity Disorder (ADHD) may have problems focusing in the classroom as well as difficulty remaining still. They may also behave impulsively or talk out of turn. Such behaviors can be frustrating for a teacher who is trying to teach while also maintaining order in the classroom. Oftentimes punitive measures are ineffective and will not help a student learn different behaviors. An alternative approach might be to engage the student separately, away from other students. At almost any age, a one-on-one discussion with a child can be rewarding for both parties. Seeing the child's struggles, through their eyes, might prompt a different strategy. A Goodness of Fit approach might be to "call on the student" more frequently so they have opportunities to speak at appropriate times. The teacher could also have a private "code" to support the student at certain times and remind them to have better self-control. There are a multitude of other creative approaches that can help the child succeed. We do not need to punish or take away another person's uniqueness.

Adjusting Cooperative Skills While Maintaining the Core Self

An important factor in helping a child succeed is the willingness to work with them and not try to change their Core Self. It is important to see every person as an individual. Children may have particular difficulties needing support and attention, but they may also struggle when feeling forced to be someone they are not. This relates more to temperament issues and unique qualities that partially define the individual's personality. Even when certain temperament classification types may be labeled under single headings or specific descriptors, no two similarly labeled temperaments should be viewed as exactly alike.

Someone considered to be Difficult as a child may grow up and maintain various aspects of this temperament type from earlier years. As an adult, they may have adjustment problems in new environments and feel intense emotional reactions to difficult situations. With an awareness of this being a repeated struggle during each stage of development, could it be helpful to guide or encourage this person to behaviorally change certain aspects of their approach to life? This could be done with children, adolescents, young adults, and older adults by acknowledging their struggle and then supportively helping them overcome their anxiety or discomfort. Can they learn alternative options to getting along with others or even experience cooperative interactions among different age groups and types of people? This may be a compassionate approach in guidance, through other options to handling daily social skills. The goal is not to change the individual but, rather, assist them in using positive skills to improve their ability to connect with others. When taught properly, a Difficult child may be guided more positively through alternative behaviors and encouragement.

A ten-year-old boy was referred to me due to depressive symptoms. His parents were concerned about his social withdrawal, isolation, and sad affect. Through minimal time talking to him, it was apparent that the chief source of his depression developed out of his struggle to make friends. Historically, he had the temperament type of a Difficult child. In his earliest years, he was described as fussy. As a toddler, he would often cry when introduced to new things or different settings. Overall, he had problems adapting to people and engaging in new situations. It was best to acknowledge his natural approach to life, but we also looked at how this approach increased his stress. This stress was interfering with his desire to make friends. Eventually, he was able to minimize his difficulties by learning new ways of engaging with other children when it felt comfortable to do so. Even though he was moving out of his comfort zone, he was aware of his greater need to develop peer friendships. There was success with this approach. Similar approaches have also been accomplished with adolescents and adults.

Each temperament type has its own strengths and weaknesses. We have the opportunity to embrace our positive qualities as well as have the freedom to work to improve parts of our temperament to gain healthy development. This can be fueled by personal insights and the choice to want positive change. As discussed earlier, our temperament remains stable over time, since it is a deeper part of the Core Self and has existed within us since birth. However, having personal awareness along with a desire to be our best can enable us to edit the less functional aspects of our temperament. This ultimately improves self-image and can motivate us to support the uniqueness of others.

Knowing and appreciating our own temperament is of value, but it is also beneficial to consider the temperament types of others. This will enable us to have better understanding, tolerance, and acceptance for all people. This also aids us to have patience with those who present in ways that do not easily match our own temperament. This approach to life should also add to the advocacy of social interest. A temperament does not define us, but having a thoughtful awareness about human differences and the importance of the various typologies can bring us closer to understanding who we are.

Components of the Self

The four temperaments theories categorize individuals using general descriptors, thus missing the distinctive qualities present in each person. Temperament alone, or its role in influencing traits, is not meant to be viewed as a personality type descriptor but a source to help us understand the progression of our personality development. If we are thinking solely in terms of the four temperaments categories, we may inadvertently lose the understanding of an individual's complexity. What is missing is the quiddity element and essence of who we are as human beings.

We are born with a temperament that influences our dominant and non-dominant traits. We are also affected by our genetics, culture, environment, and life experiences that ultimately help determine our personality. But what are those exceptional, indescribable distinguishing features that make each of us so unique? Do they come from what Plato or Aristotle referred to as the soul? Is our soul merely the breath of life or does it have spiritual properties that influence who we are as individuals? Further, how does this relate to our Core Self?

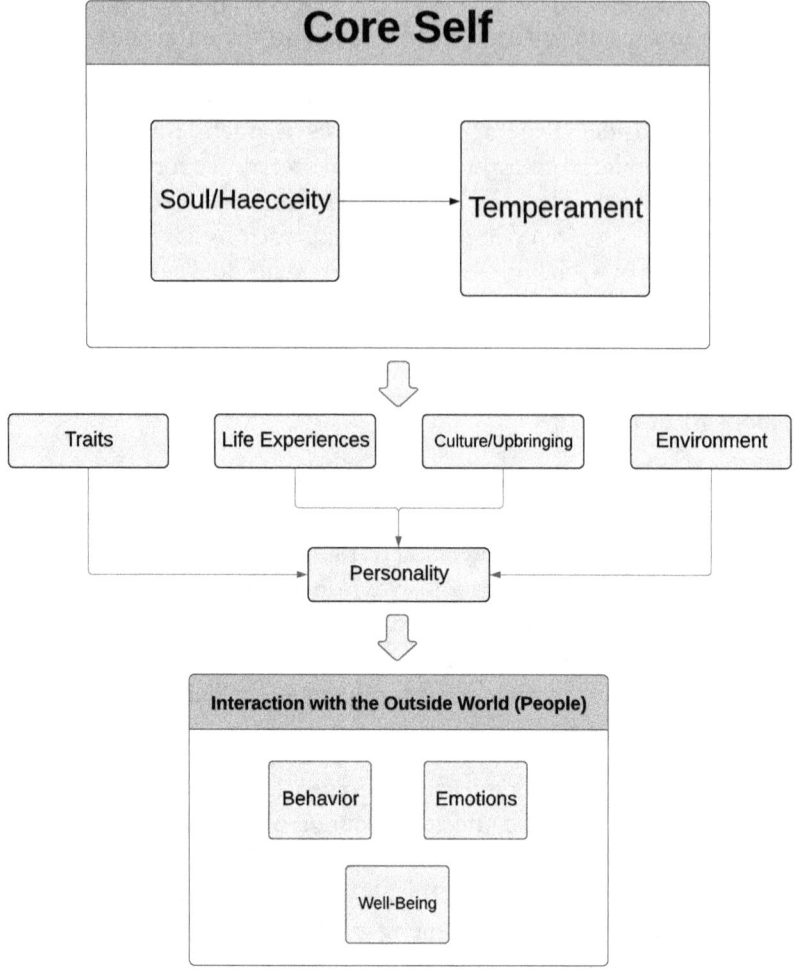

Figure 2. Total Self personality.

An important feature in Figure 2 is the continuum, moving from top to bottom. The movement starts with an abstract concept of the soul, assumed to be present in the Self, and progresses toward more definable and clearer parts of the Self that are better defined and even measurable. The Core Self is something we are born with and influences the way we think, feel, and behave. The deepest part of the Self (top of the figure) is what ancient philosophers termed the soul, that part of the Self that is the essence of our being and yet misses concrete understanding. In this model, I refer to the soul as haecceity. It is most difficult to define but is clearly present and conceivably the deepest part of the Self. Temperament is also hard to define as a specific label or personality type. It too is abstract but not to the extent of the soul. Temperaments partially explain personality but are more an early form of a person's inherent qualities of Self or disposition.

Our Core Self then has an effect upon our overall character. It influences us in relation to our traits, life experiences, culture/upbringing, and environmental factors. All of these variables are intertwined and become consolidated; personality is developed. Personality ultimately impacts our behaviors, emotions, sense of well-being, and our social interactions with the outside world.

Chapter 4

Understanding Self Types

What if I were to tell you not to change yourself? Even as a therapist, whose intentions and goals of therapy are focused on helping others make personal change in their lives, I say: Do not change who you are. This may appear to be a contradiction, due to a belief that success in therapy occurs when individuals generate change within themselves. However, change can be quite powerful when it directly relates to editing an individual's maladaptive behaviors but not censoring their own personality traits or qualities.

Insight into who we are as individuals is important. Self-acceptance is critical as we become aware of our Core Self. With this level of internal understanding we can present ourselves more genuinely to other people and navigate our communications in more honest ways. This direction creates a better likelihood that we will experience positive social interactions that can improve our lives, as we become more self-confident and happier individuals. When we present with a healthy and Real Self, we may acquire more positive and harmonious relationships with others, especially with family members, friends, or other significant social acquaintances.

Learning who we are as individuals is a critical step in the process of self-acceptance. It is our Core Self that needs to be explored. Accepting who we are, as well as accepting the uniqueness of others, is an essential goal of Core Self Theory. It has an absence of both self-judgment and negative criticism toward others. When such hurtful actions are removed, a universal acceptance will permeate every relationship we develop. Ultimately, our interactions become positive experiences with appropriate thoughtfulness and mutual consideration so that we may also experience the same goodness that we give to others.

The Core Self is the ultimate version of our Real Self. Knowing and accepting our Core Self allows us to feel free, with the likelihood of being uninhibited and honest. The Core Self is who you are currently and who you were from the past as an individual. Part of what makes you unique is that no one has your combination of traits nor their level of intensity. It is also important to consider there are core parts of yourself that have been present and unchanged since your early childhood. Behavioral reactions to people and events may change over time, but these are simply conditioned social reactions and are not necessarily genuine emotional reactions.

Our response to a particular stressor or simple event can appear to be different from our response in the past, since we have matured over time or may have learned certain acceptable reactions through social norms. If we explore a little deeper within ourselves, we might recognize familiar feelings that were present from our youth yet seem to be erased. It may appear as though we have removed the true emotional reactive quality of ourselves for the sake of assimilation or joining a group's underlining code to not convey controversial thoughts, feelings, or opinions. Should one offer different perspectives or simply share nonmainstream expressions over some topic or issue, there may be the risk of negative repercussions from the group.

If we strive to understand our Core Self and accept our own internal, genuine feelings, we can begin to experience harmony between our behavior and our Real Self rather than continue the disaffirmation from our Hidden Self or creating a Lost Self. This self-exploration is not entirely a matter of recalling past memories with associated feelings and relating them to the present. Instead, it is embracing more primitive and natural reactions rather than calculated, orchestrated behavioral communications that can become a reflex type reaction. These mechanical responses can easily become a new form of comfort, since our edited response appears less awkward and non-controversial, thus more acceptable within our social groups. If we can stop our rapid mind manipulations telling us how to respond to situations and then let there be a flow of internal natural emotions, we might recognize a person who has been hiding. We might see the face of a child who once knew how it felt when they experienced stress or joy, and they expressed it freely.

Defining the Different Self Presentations

So how do we gain insight into who our Core Self actually is? Once we have this awareness, can we manage our different self-states? Before delving deeper into these important questions, we must first understand the influencing factors disrupting Core Self comfort and the varied mentalities that impact a person's social presentation.

Below are brief definitions describing Core Self Theory and the versions of the Self that may appear. These terms are meant to convey to the reader specific differences between self-states:

Core Self Theory: A therapeutic model developed to help us understand and accept ourselves and each other as unique human beings. Core Self Theory has different applications, each with a common goal of being reality based without judgment. As a personal growth model, it focuses on self-understanding with an ultimate movement toward self-acceptance. Socially, it impacts our willingness to understand and accept the distinct differences among other people. Lastly, as a therapeutic tool, it may be used by counselors and therapists to support increased insight to help guide clients to gain deeper self-understanding, coupled with confidence building within safe boundaries. Accepting who we are and accepting the uniqueness of others is an important element of Core Self Theory.

Core Self: The deep inner self that is within us and is always present. It involves our personal emotions that guide our natural reactions to stimuli. It includes our internal uninhibited feelings that are genuine and not shaped or influenced by the praise or criticism of others. It consists of our temperament and emotions that are uniquely bundled together and unlike anyone else's. It is who you were, are, and will always be. (*Deep Inner Self—The Soul*)

Types of Selves

Lost Self: A mental process of complying with another person's, or a dominant group's, belief system, ultimately pushing true thoughts and feelings away from the conscious mind. On the surface, an individual might falsely express themselves and be unaware of their self-incongruence. However, the reward of social acceptance maintains this incompatibility on a deeper level. The end result is likely to be a routine or reflexive reaction of self-denial of true internal feelings and beliefs. In this state, the option of choosing honest responses or reactions becomes minimized, since untruthful presentations are unconsciously reinforced for social agreeability. (*Repressed Self-Fidelity—Denial*)

A representation that typifies the Lost Self is illustrated in the following example of an individual who does not socially exercise leadership qualities and is comfortable engaging in a group's space without "standing out" or appearing as different. This person appears content in carrying the group's values and opinions. This person has a high need to be accepted and has not properly evaluated their own stance or beliefs, aside from those of the group, on given topics. This is someone who has difficulty identifying issues that do not match with their own thoughts and feelings. Instead, their real feelings are repressed, since they are really unaware of their own compliance to others' values and opinions.

If questioned on an individual basis, this person would likely share the rhetoric composed by their group affiliation. At this Lost level of unawareness, the person does not know themselves or has little to no insight. Instead, this person allows others to define their identity. They are followers with little ambition and frequently feel confused about the behavior of others toward them, since each person they come in contact with has a different agenda for them and continually redefines their identity. Subconsciously, they have other views that are buried deep down and out of conscious awareness. Unfortunately, there can be internal conflict and emotional struggles due to contradictory thoughts and feelings. When our Core Self experiences one thing and our actions portray something different, we lack genuineness and feel incongruent with ourselves.

Hidden Self: The part of the Self that consciously suppresses the mind's true reaction to a given situation. It is the part of the Self that is uncomfortable revealing inner thoughts and feelings. Its purpose is to feel emotionally safe. It aims to protect us from the criticism and dismissiveness expressed to us by others. (*Guarded Self-Concealment—Avoidance*)

With this appearance of the Hidden Self, the individual is not willing to embrace their own inner thoughts and feelings. This person leans toward the direction of joining with popular ideas and withholds their own. This can occur even when the person knows they are actually opposed or have slightly varied views from what is communicated by the group in general. Though they have greater self-awareness than someone in a Lost Self state, they too deny their Core Self. Through knowing and not welcoming their own personal views, they may feel a false sense of safety due to little or no confrontation from group members.

It is unlikely that this person will openly assert themself. Their suppressed feelings are conscious but hidden, which creates a self-esteem struggle impacting mood. This person may experience various levels of discomfort, since they are more likely to have conflicting ideas that differ from the group consensus. If other people's opinions and actions take precedence over the Self's personal inclinations, the likelihood of anxiousness and depressive symptoms can emerge due to the acute feelings of incongruity.

Real Self: An open and aware person with self-acceptance. When we know and accept who we really are, we are prepared to think and express ourselves freely. It is the deeper aspect of the Core Self that is unmasked. This person accepts their own internal reactions to people, environments, and situations, and they do not align with unwanted outside influences. When we know and accept our Core Self, we experience self-clarity, with the freedom to be honest and uninhibited with our feelings. (*Internally Aware—Self-Enlightened*)

These individuals are accepting of others while maintaining their own self-awareness. For example, such a person can be in the presence of others who carry views that are in contrast to their own yet will not experience a strong compulsion to support or align with the generally accepted views. Internally, this person can maintain their own identity and feel minimal pressure to align with popular group perspectives or judgments. This person is confident with whom they are and how they feel. They may reveal their inner thoughts when asked or if encouraged; however, they will typically process personal thoughts internally.

This person is real because they do not deny their personal emotional reactions to stimuli nor do they edit their opinions based on the underlying pressures of group conformity. They are at one with themself, and they are in a state of positive mental health. Here they are generally free from anxiety and can feel confident with who they are. There is no desire to change the inner Core Self, yet they understand the value of accepting social order and certain norms or mores. They can still be themself without being oppositional or infringing on other people's rights.

Honest Self: A healthy individual with personal insight who is open and shares socially with sincerity. Such a person communicates actual thoughts and feelings without embarrassment or discomfort. With such internal awareness, we can present ourselves more genuinely, and we are more likely to develop positive social interactions with others. This person has a self-accepting outward presentation. (*Openly Revealed—Self-Sharing*)

When we are our Honest Self, we are closest to being our Core Self. As an Honest Self, we not only experience congruent thoughts and feelings but also behave accordingly with low levels of inhibition. The first person who comes to mind is my grandmother Dorothy. A very general description of Dorothy is a person who was autonomous and self-sufficient yet enjoyed spending time socially with friends and family. She was well read and educated but without degrees in higher education. She worked hard most of her life and managed to be at peace with the few fine things she acquired. She experienced various life struggles that resulted in significant life-changing decisions. She was positive and nonjudgmental.

She was once described by a psychologist friend as a woman who is truly "self-actualized." This compliment essentially meant that she had a well-developed self-awareness combined with an open acceptance of others. It also meant she met her own full potential of her abilities with a positive appreciation of life. She had an internal focus that included personal growth without experiencing overconcern about the opinions held by others. This type of growth is also true of those who are in tune with the elements of their Core Self. As this applies to Dorothy, she was at peace with herself. She could enjoy simple life experiences and attribute personal meaning to them.

In her own personal time, Dorothy was a writer and a poet who expressed feelings in a most colorful way. She could recall poems from her mid to late adulthood as well as older poems she memorized during her early youth. She might recite these poems at various times of stress. On other occasions she would recite just to savor beautiful moments in time, which paralleled the experience everyone present was feeling.

I recall one such gathering when my grandmother Dorothy visited my family with friends for dinner. As I poured glasses of wine, the table was busy with multiple conversations. Dorothy raised her wine glass in the midst of chaotic interactions between children and adults of all age levels. She began to recite a poem about wine. The words she shared encompassed the beauty of life and the significance of our all being together. My most striking memory of that moment was the eventual calm silence among us all. What presented as awkward timing was perfect timing. What seemed quiet and unheard was clear and filled with sound. What appeared to create a wince by all resulted in respectful appreciation. She spoke and was heard. The choice to express herself as she felt, specific to that moment, was pure and emanated from her Honest Self.

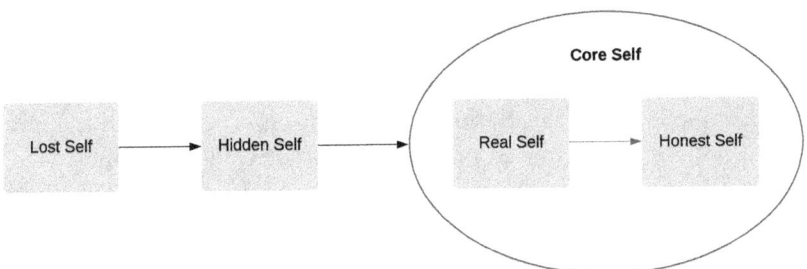

Figure 3. Lowest to highest levels of Core Self acceptance.

The above diagram in Figure 3 shows the four levels of the Self as a continuum. The lowest level of Self is the Lost Self with higher levels moving in a direction of better self-understanding and self-acceptance. The Honest Self is almost synonymous with Core Self, since this person is free from negative self-judgments and comfortably shares positively with others without guardedness and with little inhibition. This however does not dismiss the importance of realizing that there is self-knowledge also present for the two middle categories. The Hidden Self may have self-awareness but conceals it to align with others. The Real Self has that same awareness but chooses to select the parts of themself to reveal, based on their judgment of the importance and appropriateness of the situation.

When the diagram is placed in a reverse order, the sequence can be viewed as a progression of the Core Self from birth to our later years in relation to external shaping. Oftentimes, people may change their authentic, reactive self-experiences into something less recognizable to become more of a Hidden or Lost Self, however their lives begin with pure honesty as their Core Self. If the Honest Self is maintained, or reemerges over time, it is closest to our Core Self. This person feels and reacts to stimuli and social situations in a most natural, genuine manner. The Honest Self openly expresses feelings without fears of judgment or negative consequences.

Vignettes of the Various Self Types

Assuming an infant is being raised by loving, caring parents, there should be favorable reactions reinforcing the child's natural expression. In less fortunate situations, parents may be harsh in their behavior toward their child, showing low tolerance or communicating their own anxieties that can get reinforced over time. In these cases, a child develops different communication styles that may not be their natural Self.

This example is a brief illustration of a healthy child raised with the Honest Self in action. Virginia is a nine-month-old female who shows facial expressions that communicate joy, excitement, anticipation, frustration, and disinterest of the unimportant. She bangs her hands on the table in pure uninhibited enthusiasm. This emotional behavior is visceral, since she cannot verbally explain her joy. When frustrated, her cries are short lived and do not express sadness. She is gradually learning to communicate in ways that should get her needs met. Her exchanges of information come naturally, though some of her behaviors may eventually become reinforced. She is acting as her own Self.

By accident, Virginia hit herself in the head with a toy. The only emotion shown to her parents was surprise, not pain with crying. Sometimes we will see a child cry from a mild, nonhurtful body tap that worries and stirs up others; the result is usually based on expectations of how others react, as if the child is experiencing pain. But in this scenario, Virginia is behaving as her Core Self. She has the freedom to express herself naturally. At this stage of life, shaping from others may appear minimal, since it usually does not have a sudden impact. Over time, a child absorbs overt and subtle projections, beliefs, and expectations created by others around them. It is important to be aware of this as a parent, considering that shaping can be a positive as well as a negative influence over a young person over time. We want them to feel and express themself and not behave in ways that do not come naturally.

Quite the opposite can be seen with those who struggle to experience their Core Self and even fluctuate between several self-states. The shift from a natural Core Self to a denial of our own personal thoughts with true emotions creates unnatural communications and behaviors that do not match what we are actually experiencing. At times we choose to distance ourselves from our Core Self. Though it may actually seem beneficial (like being cooperative or supporting the group consensus), consciously choosing false self-presentations can have serious repercussions. When we pretend to others, it makes us false to ourselves and fake to others.

Many people can detect fakery. Some may choose to call it out directly while others choose to avoid acknowledging such observations. Sometimes it is more advantageous for observers not to comment on misrepresentations. Though one might continue operating under the guise of accepting a person's

Lost or Hidden Self, they may actually recognize false and disingenuous people and choose to give them a pass, especially when it benefits them. Also, it is sometimes easier to hear what we want to hear rather than to experience the challenge of original thoughts and new ideas.

Those who shift or fluctuate between different self-states may get so accustomed to their repositioning behavior that it becomes second nature. Such communicators learn to adapt to their environment with the appearance of agreeability and support for the consensus or person possessing the power. The habit of hiding the Real or Honest Self can become subconscious, with minimal processing. This is especially true for the Lost Self experience. When the individual consciously harbors internal thoughts and feelings to conceal their own personal process, they are acting as the Hidden Self.

In the following case, we see a presentation of a woman fluctuating between self-states in a fluid manner. At times she is aware of her inner thoughts as her Hidden Self. Other times her behavior is subconscious, and she is unaware of her Lost Self state. People commonly fluctuate between self-states but predominantly stick to one, and may alternate between two or three. Her case demonstrates a Lost Self that alternates with moments of Hidden Self awareness.

Cynthia is a forty-eight-year-old married mother of three young-adult children. She bears the responsibility of keeping the children on course and helping them build careers and develop healthy relationships. Cynthia also carries additional duties that go beyond this family. Her life is consumed with being the hub of where her family-of-origin and her extended family crossroads meet. All critical as well as superficial information passes through Cynthia. She accepts phone calls, texts, and emails to accumulate data. Whatever the subject, Cynthia has information from several angles. The obvious problem with this is that Cynthia frequently feels overwhelmed and gets placed in positions that warrant unsolicited comments and decision making, while simultaneously providing constant support and reassurance to family members that "all is well" and the "trains are running on time."

At times, Cynthia becomes stressed out and has trouble recognizing her own stance on a particular situation that is flowing through the family. Certain dyads, triads, alliances, and coalitions may develop that do not include Cynthia. However, through various other family communications she is able to perceive and recognize what is happening. She is aware of potential contentious issues that need not worry her yet draw her in as a concerned family member.

In one breath, Cynthia shares her frustration and anger with her nephew's behavior toward the grandmother. She complains to his mother (her sister) about his selfishness and lack of care, which is followed by never-ending examples of past transgressions that back her claim. In the next breath, Cynthia backpedals in an attempt to clean up the damage she created between her and her sister. Compliments for the nephew then become abundant. They are manufactured to neutralize the negative words thrown a minute earlier.

A similar example of Cynthia's behavior occurs when she complains to family members about siblings who are absent yet are needed during a crisis. Once her claims are heard by the intended family members, she pulls back. What follows are her positive statements about these individuals and their incredible helpfulness. A contradiction to her earlier statements emerge. These quality revelations are in relation to a situation that is now resolved and finished. An honest approach might have been to express her frustration over the absence of needed support during a difficult situation. No further information would be needed.

Attacking her siblings while simultaneously building them back up is either related to guilty feelings or to carrying a tinge of dishonesty and manipulation. It is possible that Cynthia felt guilty for sharing bitter feelings and criticism about her siblings. It is also possible that she was manipulatively setting up an unfavorable view of her siblings to others and then absolving herself from the responsibility of negative family reactions. After all, she seemed to provide kind words about the culprits after the damage was done.

Far from the Honest Self, Cynthia appears to fluctuate between a Lost Self and a Hidden Self. Ironically, Cynthia may see herself more as an Honest Self, since she can identify certain emotions she is experiencing and expresses her feelings freely. What is missing here is a deeper understanding of her motives and goals. Such individuals appear to be multitasking with manipulations, and they lose track of their intended communications.

Cynthia mishandled her frustration with her siblings. If she were an Honest Self, she could have shared her dissatisfaction or even anger for her siblings' poor support. Their lack of attention to the crisis meant that Cynthia had to manage things on her own. It would be her Real Self that recognizes her own level of frustration. This is a natural, internal experience she would actually feel within herself. Her choice to verbalize this with an intention of honestly sharing her internal reaction will make this an Honest Self experience.

While examining both of the above family scenarios for Cynthia, we see that she feels used and abused by family members yet places herself in this role, since she truly wants to be the nucleus of the family. Her boundaries become blurred as she works to please yet criticizes the very people she chooses to engage. She is a Lost Self since she loses her individual identity trying to be important and someone in whom others want to confide. She is Lost because she is unaware of her own malleable flexibility to conform to family members and to maintain her position as the "go-to person" with family gossip or stress. At times Cynthia is her Hidden Self when she may fluctuate between knowing and accepting her own internal reactions and feelings but also suppressing them.

Through examination of these associated self-states, we see some variations that appear subtle while other differences are more apparent. Recognize that the Core Self is an overall ideal of knowing the Self. It may further be described as the ultimate objective in self-understanding and self-acceptance. When we know our Core Self, we recognize a familiar Self that is synchronized in time, relating to past raw emotions and the freedom to think in the present with ideas that belong to you, the individual. Getting back to a place of the Real or Honest Self is challenging since there may be too much familiarity in presenting as a Lost or Hidden Self. Familiarity is comfortable, and there are also plenty of built-in rewards for behaviors that accept common trends and group solidarity. Imagine the following scenario:

Albert enjoys a leisurely moment among friends. They have finished playing in a softball tournament and are wrapping up their time together by enjoying a BBQ lunch and sharing stories about the weekend games. As the social discussion evolves, the subject matter changes. Conversations are now focused on current events and politics. Comments are shared about certain people with a critical tone. Strong opinions follow and are made in reference to political groups and affiliations. As the conversation continues, more and more support for group agreement is apparent and favors the opinions of the group's leaders.

There appear to be common viewpoints coupled with criticism, with subtle mocking of anyone holding opposite viewpoints. Albert has different opinions and is not comfortably persuaded by his friends' remarks and ideas.

Albert tries to internally process the material everyone seems to support. He uses his logic to analyze their judgments and beliefs. The friends seem to make sense as they "back up" their positions with statistics and background history, neatly packaging their conclusions, while others collude with the presented narrative. Albert is silent yet recognizes his own uneasiness due to his thought process. If asked what he believes, can he offer an honest perspective?

This situation can have several outcomes, depending on the group's mentality as well as Albert's level of sharing. It is possible that these softball buddies have a genuine interest in contrasting views and might appreciate an open exchange of ideas about differences shared. Another possibility is that such a discussion could trigger negative reactions and arguments that might alienate Albert.

If presenting as a Lost Self, Albert would automatically join the group perspective. Very little thought will be made concerning his own personal viewpoint, and Albert will support the consensus on the group's subject matters. Albert might even add a little extra information to build on previously stated points and may gain further encouragement from the group for a job well done. This subconscious process however hurts the Self. It negatively impacts his self-esteem due to the incongruence of his Core Self and what he presents to the group. His personal feelings and deeper beliefs are pushed out of conscious awareness. If he acts as a Hidden Self, Albert feels uncomfortably acquainted with his own differing viewpoints and struggles to verbalize them for fear of group rejection and ridicule. This struggle is more difficult when compared to the Lost Self, since there is an internal awareness that his perspectives are in contrast and vary in some ways to the group stance and attitude. But the Hidden Self makes a choice to conceal themself. They choose to "go along" to "get along." It feels safer to join the group rather than oppose it. Like the Hidden Self, the Real Self is also aware of their inner thoughts and feelings, but they are not actively avoiding. Instead, they are self-accepting, tuned in to their own genuine reaction to the discussed material, and comfortably own what is internally experienced. This depth of self-understanding and self-acceptance may further lead to the Honest Self, who is aware of their internal process and is able to communicate with little or no reservation. These individuals are able to express themselves genuinely. They can readily reveal their Real Self with little apprehension.

A similar situation is illustrated in this next example relating to an internal conflict of the Self. Sarah joins a group of volunteers at her children's elementary school. It is her wish to contribute and collaborate with a group of women planning their school's annual fundraising charity event. As a tradition, this activity has existed for the past ten years, and the current team of leaders have actively participated in this event for the last five years. This participation history appears to be an advantage, since these leaders understand the school's tradition along with the event goals. Since these leading women have a past work history together, they understand each other's strengths and can utilize them appropriately. In addition to Sarah's joining the group, there are other new volunteers, some with unique skills that can be utilized as refinements, constructively adding something extra to this special event.

Sarah attends preliminary volunteer meetings with the intention of co-operating with the group and assisting in areas where she is needed. The tone of the group is usually upbeat and positive. While the leaders appear grateful for Sarah's support as well as other new volunteers, they establish a clear hierarchy, placing newbies in positions of less value and minimal usefulness. On one level, Sarah appreciates the advantages of learning from experienced volunteers who take on responsibilities overseeing the event. She recognizes that their knowledge of running such an activity is invaluable. On another level, Sarah expects to contribute something personal. She hopes to strengthen the event by adding something extra that is part of an overall collective and creative process. Instead, the leadership passively dismisses new volunteers. They plan to administer the fundraiser in the same established manner as was done in previous years. There are no new ideas and there are only basic tasks delegated to new volunteers. Apparently, these are the underlying unspoken rules. To Sarah's surprise, the other new volunteers are agreeable and get placed in functions that seem insignificant. They are, however, not supported when sharing new ideas. They are discouraged from offering solutions for predicaments or problems that arise. If suggestions are made, they are gently dismissed with a return back to the leaders who retain old approaches and manage accordingly.

For Sarah, it is internally uncomfortable accepting the leaders' overall approach. She feels excluded and rejected as a team contributor. Sarah also experiences a sense of disconnect from her fellow new group members. Though they have all entered this volunteer group to be part of a positive and giving experience, there is a lack of inclusion, separating the established leaders from new members. Unfortunately, this separateness is minimized by the new volunteers and is generally accepted by them. New members seem to fall in line with the plans laid out by the individuals who are in charge. Roles are established without question. Sarah is aware of her unenthusiastic emotional reaction to this experience.

The concept of the Lost Self may explain why other group members are compliant and do not react negatively to the group leaders' plans. Maybe these individuals are in denial about true feelings of discontent. Perhaps their true emotions are shut down with the underlying hope of getting along with the group to feel some sense of approval. If Sarah is to also present as a Lost Self, she would accept the group's attitudes and perspectives. She would not allow her own personal thoughts and feelings to surface, and she would go along with the group plan, which avoids controversy. Her true feelings and honest beliefs would be pushed out of her conscious awareness. However, as a Lost Self, Sarah would likely feel unhappy and discouraged because of the incongruence between her Core Self and what she presents to the group.

If Sarah's behavior relates more to the Hidden Self, she would be leaning less to a state of denial and instead would be more inclined toward avoidance. In this condition Sarah would be consciously aware of her Core Self incongruity. This means she is stuck in a place of actively hiding her true thoughts and feelings. As the Hidden Self, she joins with the easy and acceptable group direction, while discounting what she actually wants to share. With this mentality, Sarah will internally experience a negative sense of Self, since she is giving in to something that is foreign to her inner beliefs while accepting the group assertions. Sarah might play along, with the hopes of gaining a bigger payoff over time. Maybe next year she will be more accepted and given a more prominent position among the volunteers.

Instead, Sarah is more in touch with her Real Self. She is aware of her internal thoughts and feelings through self-examination. She recognizes the unfair, biased approach managed by those who are in charge. She also sees that there is a lack of available peer support, should she choose to openly express herself. Her conflict is to determine whether it is worth the effort to present as an Honest Self. This decision is sensitive because it could disrupt the order of the volunteer community. It could also evolve into unwanted splits within their group dynamic. Conversely, with honest communication, there might be a healthier outcome. There might be an engaged group pursuing open discussion with better understanding over what Sarah, and perhaps others, might want to include in the volunteer group process. In this state, the Honest Self is free to express a positive intention without judgment fears.

Real or Honest Self: Your Choice

A decision to reveal one's Self among others with different ideas can feel risky. Here, the notion of safety becomes a serious concept that is important when considering a potential outcome after sharing honest opinions and thoughts. Such freedom of expression may result in what can seem like more harm than good. When personal viewpoints are shared but unwanted, there may be some backlash shown by either implied or obvious communications. Ultimately, there are consequences for going against the grain. In a mature person, freedom to be real or honest requires strength and assertiveness as one maintains their expressed ideas. Sometimes it may be best not to argue or debate an expressed idea. However, it could be more advantageous to help others hear and understand different perspectives.

Certainly, open and lively debates among trusted friends are low-risk exchanges of ideas. Straightforward expression is ideal in allowing the Self to be real and natural. Expressing your Core Self can feel liberating as long as the challenges from others are not meant to hurt your character or demean you as a person. True freedom of expression should evoke openness to opinions, beliefs, and viewpoints. It is not necessary that the individuals present must share the same stance or outlook for the ideas presented by another. Simply listening without judgment is what is important. Mutual acceptance for open and sincere sharing is ideal. We want to accept the Core Self of others as well.

As individuals, we are often shaped by the world around us. Sometimes we are drawn in through the influence or persuasion of others. With such a situation, low-key pressures are made that call upon others to think and behave in ways deemed socially acceptable within the group. This is a type of peer pressure commonly seen among middle school children and adolescents, but it is also experienced by other age groups and at various social statuses. There may be clear or subtle directives guiding outsiders toward the inner circle. Here, the rewards will result in peer acceptance and ultimately increase group cohesion.

If this becomes too challenging or others appear unwilling or reluctant to conform, negative consequences may appear. Sometimes personal feelings, opinions, statements, and genuine reactions do not comfortably meld with the views of the dominant group (which may also have been shaped.) Sometimes we can become compliant, ultimately giving in to the norms that direct how individuals "should" be. The treatment model of Albert Ellis (Rational Emotive Behavioral Therapy) relates to this concept. Ellis recognized that a person's irrational thinking can lead to feelings of incongruence. This is often experienced through the "musts" and "shoulds" we were raised with and that have become internalized throughout our lives, to try to live up to related expectations. The emotional reaction to such incongruity may be experienced as anxiety and depression.

Early in our lives, we may become indoctrinated with irrational thoughts reinforced by some of the significant people in our lives. These key individuals might include parents and teachers but may also involve other important authority figures from our childhood. Ellis believed that we accept certain irrational thoughts as well as create our own repetitive false or distorted beliefs. However, internal beliefs about "musts" and "shoulds" can result in unnecessary behaviors that we act on and abide by. The expectations of what we "must" or "should" do somehow guides us into irrationally behaving as a Lost Self with dissonant beliefs taking away from the Core Self.

Once we realize that our lives do not require absolute repeated or required responses regulated by others, we can relax a little, start to process our own thoughts as the Real Self, and begin to accept ourselves for who we are. This type of realization can be experienced when an individual with unique ideas or different values associates—and may join—with a particular group carrying a separate mentality. The realization may be felt in ways that are mildly noticeable, such as when an individual feels comfortable associating with a group and its dynamics yet still has internal clarity about personal opinions, such as with a Real Self experience that differs from the group.

Occasionally, unexpected differences or misunderstandings can develop among group members and might not accurately represent an individual's Real Self position. However, feeling content with personal differences accompanied by mutual acceptance can sometimes be enough. It may feel suitable to become cooperative among good people who carry views contrasting with some of our individual opinions. We may still experience congruence of the Self, considering we feel safe enough to honestly assert our limits of acceptance or disagreement with the group. Though we may not fully join with all group opinions, we may comfortably socialize since we are confident with our Real or Honest Self.

Frank is an example of a man who is comfortable with his Real Self. He may be described as sociable and well liked by most who know him. He has the ability to get along with others and fit in with various social groups, behaving like a chameleon. He is nonthreatening, nonchallenging, and open-minded. Though he maintains his own thoughts and personal identity, he simultaneously engages with others who carry different life views from his own. He has a positive approach to engaging others and assimilates within different groups, demonstrating acceptance of others while being accepted.

Frank developed several positive relationships with coworkers. Out of these relationships some closer friendships developed. Since Frank was good at listening and genuinely being present for others, he was well liked and regarded as a caring and thoughtful person. He rarely spoke about his own personal struggles, but he would share similar, parallel type experiences of himself with the intent to connect and provide subtle advice or constructive feedback. With this level of care and consideration for others, Frank became well liked by most who knew him. Eventually, through regular and close associations with certain coworkers, friendships led to frequent contacts and routine gatherings outside of work. Certain work friends met on a regular basis and became more of a social group affiliation.

The group was a partial extension of his work buddies, which felt comfortable. Frank also enjoyed the camaraderie he experienced with the group's rich level of activities. There was always something to do with ongoing gatherings that included family picnics, golf on Saturdays, and invitations to different people's homes for socializing, drinks, and dinner. Frank seemed to be affiliated with an exclusive peer group from work. This meant he was being seen among well-known and admired people and appeared generally accepted by them. Most of his close coworkers associated Frank with this favored group. Unfortunately, this group was not well liked by all. While some individuals made the effort to be connected to the group, there were unspoken rules that placed good and decent peers in a nonpermissible role of nonacceptance. Some were treated in socially negative ways, creating feelings of vulnerability and rejection by this unaccepting group.

Frank was somewhat oblivious to the separateness among coworkers. His belief in equality and being nonjudgmental was a constant state of mind, and he had open acceptance toward others. However, the problem that emerged was that Frank could not easily flow between two different camps of people. There was his newly developed group of friends with whom he enjoyed time socially, yet Frank also had positive relationships with several other work peers and chose to continue his same openness and shared communications with them.

Being a chameleon had its advantages. Frank had fluidity with openness and freedom to associate with anyone or any group he wanted. However, his positive communications were made on a one-to-one level and might not always have been the accepted or expected behavior of someone associated with the in-group. Fortunately, welcoming openness with others, regardless of their group affiliation, was behavior that suited Frank comfortably. He was free to be his Real or Honest Self with those he chose to affiliate with, while not feeling pressured or forced to choose sides.

There was no actual need to choose among friends in Frank's mind, yet a subtle sense of pressure was initiated by others. Negativity was shared by individuals about opposing groups. This was meant to persuade Frank to view these people or their group with a critical attitude. Such communications were unacceptable to Frank, and they did not convince him to change his opinion of others. In fact, he was not supportive of any form of negativity and through his Honest Self would speak of his own views, disarming others who were delivering any negative messages. In some instances, Frank was criticized and not supported for his personal choices. This was acceptable to him, considering he was clear on his personal beliefs and opinions. He was not coerced into engaging in ways that were not real and not part of his Core Self.

A variation of the same kind of preference to be one's Honest Self without pushing others away can be seen in the case of Carrie. This is someone who internally knows she is unhappy when complying with unwanted group pressures; however, she is also cognizant of her internal conflict and chooses to address it through healthy communication. Sometimes we experience inner struggles when we become aware of incongruent feelings because our ideas or values do not match with the group. There is relief in understanding that we can choose to be who we are. The challenge is accepting reactions and responses from group members, whether positive or negative.

Carrie entered a group of college peers who have all become friends. They socialize regularly, both on campus and outside their school. Lately, Carrie has felt out of place while among her friends. She has a tendency to want to please others and does not like challenges. Carrie will often join in group activities that do not interest her, yet she frequently ends up helping to coordinate and manage events, since she is known to be responsible and reliable with great organizational skills. At some point, Carrie realizes she is unhappy with the group. She finds it odd that she actually likes most all the individuals in the group, or enjoys smaller groupings of these friends, but not as the larger group and definitely not as their "go-to" person.

Carrie sought to break free of the role she assumed. She recognized she was not in tune with her Core Self. Carrie usually fluctuated between feeling as the Hidden Self and the Real Self. Though she had insight into the incongruity of feelings versus behaviors, she felt stuck in portraying herself as the person everyone else wanted to see. It was a type of peer pressure that ultimately exploited Carrie's good nature and reinforced old and uncomfortable, reflex type behaviors she was accustomed too. She would appease the others at her own cost, which made her feel like a victim and created some resentment.

Carrie began to ease into the actions of an Honest Self. She stated she felt free to "be myself" and not worry about peer reactions. If her friends were unhappy with her behavior, she felt comfortable addressing the issue. She became more assertive but never aggressive. To her surprise, the group of individuals appreciated her Honest Self. She could share her feelings about a matter when asked, and she volunteered her ideas or opposing decisions when appropriate. This was done by saying what she wanted to say and not being inhibited. This newfound freedom of expression with self-acceptance opened Carrie to further opportunities in her life to share honestly among various groups of people. An added bonus was the deeper introspection with self-discovery she made, allowing her to become more aware of her Core Self.

Learning to speak with one's own voice is essential in the growth between one's Lost Self and Honest Self. While not all groups push others toward conformity, it is refreshing to know that some individuals can experience acceptance regardless of having different thoughts, values, or ideas. In some instances, individuals or groups may encourage others to feel free to be themselves. It is ideal when we are among people who support individuality while not being judgmental. For some, it is still very difficult to assert personal thoughts and feelings that vary from a group's consensus. Here, it may feel safer to be guarded while carrying the role of a Hidden Self. Conversely, it might take courage to engage others with unfettered openness, especially when it is not being supported. Under these circumstances, one might feel challenged by expectations set by certain individuals or a group of people. It is at these times when courage may be significant, considering a possible social penalty of shunning or ostracization. However, there is still a high level of self-satisfaction that comes from being the person you really are.

Sharing oneself honestly is a positive goal. While it is important to express yourself with an open mind, it is also necessary to be aware of other people's personal views, even when they differ from your own. Such free and open expressiveness becomes a fair exchange of ideas. This should increase the likelihood of mutual acceptance. Sometimes when we surround ourselves with healthy people who are open to differences and accepting of others, there is freedom to express ourself naturally and unselfconsciously.

Unfortunately, we may find ourselves in the company of some who purposely or subconsciously aim to change the Self that we present genuinely. When this occurs, it is reasonable to pull back and assess our inner feelings. If an uneasy reaction is felt, we may want to recalibrate and approach others differently. Sometimes we might feel it is beneficial to minimally engage and avoid the unsupportive environment. At other times we may still maintain our Real or Honest Self while receiving only small amounts of negative feedback. Below are some examples of this struggle to choose different behaviors that may or may not be congruent with the Real or Honest Self.

Emily reflects on her past relationships in which she became stuck in a pattern that allowed men to disregard how she wanted to present herself to the outside world. Because of this influence, she usually felt uncomfortable or unsafe when disclosing personal ideas and views. She withheld expressing her real feelings. In her relationships, her partners could partially discount elements of her Core Self. She was stuck somewhere between a Lost Self and a Hidden Self. However, now she is working on self-acceptance.

In her current relationship, she feels more confident having the freedom to express herself without fear of reprisal, as she did in previous relationships. She is striving toward honest expression yet is uneasy about this due to past relationship experiences. An interesting element in her success of becoming an Honest Self is the support felt from within this healthier relationship. The support essentially equates to providing safety for Emily to reveal herself and feeling confident in knowing her own values, not someone else's.

Emily's story is an interesting example of moving from a Lost Self to a Real Self. Emily was conditioned by early life experiences that taught her to repress her Core Self. There were trust and safety issues related to her discomfort with individuality. This partially explains why certain males were able to influence or control her to the point of accepting their directives to gain their approval. Through understanding her own patterns of behavior, she acknowledged a repetitive cycle of struggling to assert herself. This allowed her to distance herself from her most recent unhealthy relationship while working on reconnecting with her Core Self. Over time, Emily engaged in actions that gave her opportunities to be real. Her choices in friendships were healthier, and her relationship was more open and honest, with clear freedom to express and be as she felt most comfortable.

In other life circumstances, a reverse of Emily's experience can occur. This is true for certain individuals who sincerely strive to be their Core Self, yet become forced into Hidden Self behavior. Such individuals are most comfortable with their freedom to be a Real or Honest Self, yet feel forced into denying themselves the relief felt in Core Self experiences. Their behavior change becomes a last resort to manage feelings that should normally appear positive and open. Under normal circumstances, this person is comfortable expressing themselves with little inhibition. They are able to share thoughts and feelings freely until they are compelled to behave out of character. This usually appears following major stress from some unmanageable outcomes delivered by a mean-spirited person or group of small-minded people. A clear instance of this type of negative transformation is illustrated in the following example.

James is a man described as being "full of life." He is genuine and caring toward the people he loves. He also is known as a person who helps others in need. James may be classified as an extrovert. He enjoys socializing and usually initiates conversations with those he meets for the first time. He engages in light, fun conversation but also connects through deeper meaningful discussions. James is uninhibited when sharing his opinions. He speaks honestly, while being open to others with different viewpoints. He is not reserved and is straightforward when communicating. James feels free to be his Core Self.

James has a small law firm that covers estate planning and family law matters. He is independent but has a great network of friends who receive client referrals based on their specializations and expertise. Such referrals benefit James's clientele, since he knows and trusts his referral base's quality of work. He also has an open line of communication with these referral friends and comfortably makes contact with them as he works for the best interest of his clients. Occasionally, these friends refer clients to James, and the same principle of shared communication works out for the benefit of the client.

A new young attorney established a law practice in James's same office building. Though they had separate practices, they could benefit from each other through consultation and sharing legal matters of common interest. Sometimes they had business lunches together, often including James's referral source friends. They were friendly and open to referring to each other. This depended on whether a client could benefit more from one of these attorney's strengths and be a better fit within their scope of practice.

James arrived at work one day and observed one of his clients entering the building. Instead of meeting with James, the client went to the office of his attorney friend. Later in the day, James inquired about the client's visit. The attorney friend shared that he was helping the client with some legal matters, separate from James's work with them. As James explored the issue further, the attorney friend became defensive. He resisted a cordial discussion regarding the matter and behaved in a quarrelsome manner. At a minimum, it would have been appropriate for him to show understanding. He could have explained the client's needs or possible desire to make a shift in attorney representation. Instead, he reacted with bitterness and angrily became confrontational.

Beyond the hostile exchange, other negative actions by the attorney friend started to follow. For example, he began to separately develop relationships with the referral friend network that James had created. It soon became apparent that clients and referral sources were aggressively being pulled from this network. As James discovered this attorney's covert behaviors, he pulled back and changed his approach when interacting with the attorney friend. This approach was also present among certain professionals within his referral group of friends.

After this series of events, James felt a need to pull away from the attorney friend and became restrained in his usual positive, expressive Self. He recognized that he felt hurt and betrayed. Instead of showing his typical free and open personality in the company of the attorney friend, he became quiet, with a toned-down presence. This was not because he was emotionally wounded. It was a conscious choice to pull away from this person. He lessened his Honest Self, containing his emotions by becoming a Hidden Self. James was no longer comfortable as his Core Self in the presence of the attorney friend. He stated, "I feel forced to be distant, cold, and defensive; I'm unkind instead of being giving, caring, social, and positive."

The option of choosing to restrain elements of the Core Self in stressful situations may occur as a conscious solution that is self-protective. The alternative could be to behave as the Real or Honest Self, however there may be little value in exposing oneself to the emotional harms of rejection and mistreatment from others who are hostile. Unfriendly communications from negative individuals or groups may be a painful experience that increases psychological vulnerability. Though it is not wise to ignore hostility or harsh communications from others, it is wiser to be alert, recognizing the value of proper timing when speaking your mind. In other words, it is psychologically satisfying to feel free and open, sharing one's thoughts and feelings with pure sincerity. However, when there are foreseeable negative repercussions from honesty within certain social interactions, be perceptive and cautious with your social expressiveness.

Chapter 5

Positive and Negative Traits of Self

It is important to embrace who we are in totality. Realistically, we carry both positive and negative traits that are influenced by our temperament and social surroundings. While it is ideal to have all positive traits, we possess other traits that do not present so positively. These less positive traits may unexpectedly create interpersonal problems when conveyed to others without some sort of altering.

In actuality, a single trait may carry both positive and negative aspects. It is wise to have this awareness. Mindful communication with appropriate reframing may be sensible and probably in the best interest of a relationship. This is an important factor to recognize, especially when one begins to feel empowered to fully be themself. While being one's Self is about being real and honest, we must also be cognizant of how being our Honest Self can impact others.

When looking into our true selves at an early age, we may recognize both positive and negative features of the Self that exist internally. Some of these Core Self features are also observed by others. Depending on the characteristic, they may also experience it as a positive or negative element of the Self. Traits that we carry innately appear to have some type of variability in terms of how they get presented to others. Understanding our traits may require deeper self-analysis to determine how they are influenced by our temperament and by the essence of our Self.

Reworking Negative Traits

Through this deeper realization we will discover exceptional traits that we want to maintain and share with others. On the other hand, we might also discover having some undesirable traits that have existed since the earliest stages of our lives, and as such they are components of the Core Self that we must accept and acknowledge as also genuine parts of ourselves. Not an easy task, but once this is accomplished, the challenge becomes the ability to learn suitable and fitting communication of a negative trait that is presented with a constructive mindset. It is a productive and beneficial approach when we accept who we are and can be cognizant of our negative traits that might produce behavior that is not helpful to ourselves and others.

For example, some of us have an active negative trait of *jealousy*. Let us suppose we explored this trait within our own lives going back to an early age. Perhaps we continuously struggled with this trait from the past up to the present, recognizing there were accompanying negative feelings that we experienced internally. Feeling jealous may have made us feel insecure, unworthy, or incompetent in our lives. Even our self-esteem may have dropped due to deeper feelings of inadequacy with frustration and anger toward another person. Such feelings are uncomfortable and unwanted. Working on one's Self to manage such emotions may seem improbable, but it is actually manageable. A helpful and productive outcome will depend on how we choose to process our thoughts and feelings. It will be especially beneficial if our mindset is purposely open to alternative views when reframing the negative.

First, we should not be in denial of the trait and how it makes us feel. Accepting jealousy as a part of our Real Self helps us understand ourselves, since we are in touch with our feelings. We do not want to have internal conflict over such things as being right or wrong/good or bad. Once we have this self-acceptance, our feelings may still lead us into further negativity. This might include related behaviors that can negatively affect the people around us. This negative trait will also lead to our own negative feelings. Our negative feelings may unleash negative actions that ultimately hurt others or push people away. This is an undesirable outcome that can be changed into something more favorable and still be part of the Real Self. The progression of a trait having a negative social outcome is presented below.

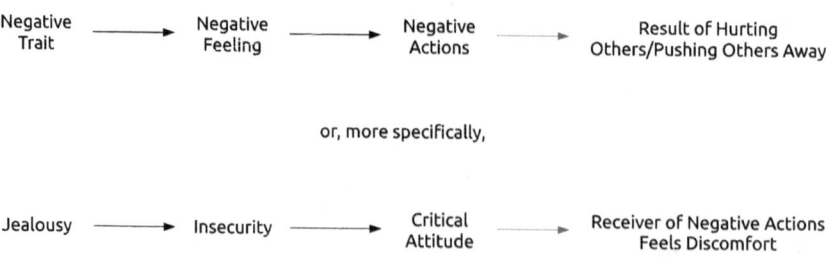

Negative Trait	⟶	Negative Feeling	⟶	Negative Actions	⟶	Result of Hurting Others/Pushing Others Away

or, more specifically,

Jealousy	⟶	Insecurity	⟶	Critical Attitude	⟶	Receiver of Negative Actions Feels Discomfort

After accepting the unwanted feeling, subsequent behavior, and outcome of our own negative trait, we become open to exploring alternative perspectives of what this trait might hold outside of general negativity. We must recognize other trait factors that can be defined as positive and useful. The important consideration is that we can process a trait through different options. For example, could my struggles with jealousy allow me to have compassion for others like myself, or could my jealousies transform into internal motivation to push me to achieve things I might not have thought to pursue? These would be productive experiences with the trait of jealousy that are positive.

Another illustration of a reframed negative self-characteristic that includes different positive options is the trait of *stubbornness*. By definition, a stubborn person struggles with change, such as with an attitude or a position on an issue. Stubbornness is likely seen as a trait that shows low cooperation with a lack of reciprocal communication. Stubborn individuals tend to resist different ideas and may refuse to accept alternative choices. This negative trait may create a feeling of being rigid, stuck, or alone. It also lacks support from others and may decrease such things as teamwork and unity. As a result, a bout with stubbornness may end with arguments and pushing others away. The progression of this trait's having a negative social outcome is presented below.

Stubbornness ──→ Rigidness ──→ Resistance ──→ Inconsideration of Other People's Feelings

Stubbornness as a trait can be reframed with a more positive association. Being considered steadfast, committed, and loyal are all attributes related to stubbornness. They are alternative views of what is usually presented as negative. Such a person certainly carries strength in their convictions, and they are willing to assert themself. They might present as decisive, tenacious, persistent, and not giving up easily. Here, the trait has converted from something typically experienced as negative into something that is positive, especially when communicated effectively and for useful purposes.

Resentfulness is another common but unpleasant trait that is experienced by many. There are usually continual recurrent feelings that arise when thinking about issues of resentment. The associated negative feelings may be helplessness, hopelessness, impotent rage, a deep sense of unfairness, victimhood, and anger toward the Self for allowing others to mistreat them with no apparent consequences. Such thoughts and feelings are difficult to stop, and they feed into the negative trait. This is frustrating and can create problems related to a negative self-image. It also increases an emotional separation between those who might trigger the resentment and the person who is the object of the negative experience.

Resentfulness ⟶ Injustice ⟶ Anger ⟶ Distance in Communication

This trait is difficult to reframe into positive characteristics. Upon reflection we may recognize that a resentful person may also carry the belief that it is in their power to control and affect how others treat them, and yet they still have failed to do so and their failure caused the other person to completely mistreat them. What a resentful person can learn or understand from this negative feeling is that within them there is a belief that may be cognitively distorted. They can begin to learn to accept that they may have an erroneous belief but not go along with the self-criticism that comes with it.

It is really not in our power to control how others treat us or feel about us. It is, however, in our power to recognize when we have not been treated as well as we feel that we deserve. This new awareness and acceptance will release the resentful person from the self-anger that they somehow allowed the mistreatment to happen when it really was out of their hands. With the absence of this negative self-view, resentment can instead create empathy toward others who have experienced injustice, and it can teach the troubled person acceptance of their limited power over others.

Certain negative traits are accompanied by strong emotions that have a clear impact on others. Perhaps the trait of *impatience* evokes certain common emotions felt by most individuals. A person's irritability and restlessness may be communicated when the trait is expressed rather than internally managed. The resultant reaction felt by others creates more negativity rather than productive and respectful exchanges.

Impatience ⟶ Frustration ⟶ Dissatisfaction ⟶ Lack of Support

A more constructive approach to managing this negative trait is to have an awareness of how one's own impatience may be modified by acknowledging that it is more beneficial and effective to get things done in a proper and timely manner rather than in haste. The automatic, reflexive feeling of impatience can be managed in a way that does not push others away nor create increased negativity. While it is perfectly appropriate to experience impatience with its accompanying emotions, there are other variables to take into consideration. For instance, the timing of our expression of impatience and how it gets communicated might be inappropriate. The physical surroundings and the people present may also be a consideration when expressing the feelings accompanying the trait. In such circumstances, an impatient impulse may actually be hurtful to some people, yet not distressing to others.

Even though we all carry both negative and positive traits, our social interactions benefit by looking at how personal negative traits can be acknowledged and how we may work with them. We do not want our negative traits to heavily appear and dominate our lives, even though they come from a natural part of our Core Self. Instead, we want to acknowledge and define those parts of ourselves. This process increases our self-awareness and brings us closer to the Real Self.

With this, we may be presenting the Self in ways that might allow us to join with others rather than push them away. Therapeutically, it opens up our inner self to better connect with others while not abandoning the inner part of our Core Self. This awareness is the first step toward managing negative traits. Ideally, we will want to recognize negative emotions that are repeatedly triggered, then consciously decide how to manage them.

Thoughtful Concerns While Being Real

It is important to be aware of two things: the Self and others. Certainly, it is ideal to have the freedom to think and behave as naturally as one can be, without social constraints or limits that prevent us to grow with Core Self freedom. However, we must also have insight as well as self-control and be aware of our impact on those around us. Being one's Core Self does not mean selfishness. Instead it is a place of self-understanding, where a person will not deny who they are nor what they believe.

Behaving as one's Core Self also means there is a respect for others, even when there are varied and obvious differences. When among others with diverse ideas, it is best to choose an honest, appropriate approach. This could be addressing the other(s) nonoffensively by stating a different point of view, confronting the difference directly without avoidance, maintaining silence and not engaging or giving in, and complying with an opposite opinion.

These are options that most of us encounter frequently. The choice will depend on the particular circumstance, but it is best to be aware of the Real Self at all times and not give in to something that goes against who we are.

Questions we may ask ourselves: "If I am to be my Core Self but my behavior/communication infringes on another person's freedom, what is the healthy approach?" This might occur when we verbalize a thought or idea that clearly opposes another person's beliefs or opinions. While this could be healthy banter on some occasions, it may also appear as unsupportive and even challenging under other circumstances.

A similar yet different question to decipher: "If I am to be my Core Self but my behavior presents as odd, inappropriate, or goes against social norms, what is the healthy approach for such situations?" In these circumstances, we would want to have the insight as to how a particular communication comes across to others. This might occur if I present to others as unedited in my need to express myself.

If I can predict a negative outcome by communicating as my Honest Self, or if I am able to recognize when I am not being positively received, I may want to change my approach. Changing an approach toward others does not mean I abandon my Core Self. Instead, it is a means of communicating diplomatically or a form of respecting the views of others. The Real Self is intact while the choice to express oneself freely is a decision that may be based on expected outcomes.

The management of our own communications has benefits and can lessen the unfortunate possibility of misunderstandings or unnecessary conflict. The value of knowing our Core Self has great worth. It increases insight into ourselves while not leading to thoughts and feelings being recklessly expressed anytime and anywhere. This may be observed personally or in a greater social context. For example, breaking the law and claiming in court that your violation of the law was simply a Core Self behavior will not excuse the crime or lower the sentence. We need to be conscious of others and manage our thoughts and behaviors appropriately. Poor impulse control is a lack of the ability to edit the Self in specific situations. Having the awareness of the Core Self is most important, but behaving in a congruent manner is secondary and takes several questions into consideration.

1. Could my honest expressiveness and behavior negatively affect others?
2. Will my behavior go against social norms?
3. Can my behavior be construed as odd, selfish, or offensive, thus making other people distance themselves from me?

These items are the types of questions that can ideally be processed spontaneously before acting publicly/socially as one's Core Self. As an example, a male client shared his honest approach to others and how he always "spoke out" about what was on his mind. He admitted that he did not always hold the popular views shared by others, but he was quick to step up and state his opinion for the given subject. The obvious Core Self advantage was that he was free to express himself in the most honest and congruent way. The problem was that the aftereffects of his repeated approach ultimately limited his number of friendships. Coworkers, acquaintances, and family members seemed to be cautious around him, and he felt the distance. Though he was defensive about how his Honest Self communication was best for himself, he also recognized that his approach often dealt with the considerations listed above. Though he was not very concerned about going against social norms, he actually wanted to positively connect with others and not be viewed negatively.

Another example is a 12-year-old client who was emotionally regressed and baby-like. His parents reported that he was bullied at school and alienated within their larger extended family of cousins, aunts, and uncles due to his bizarre antics. He cried when he did not get his way, he screamed and jumped up and down when he was excited, and he made strange and funny noises that amused himself but bothered the people around him. As a result he was depressed because many significant people in his life rejected him. Was this fair? He was actually behaving in ways that felt natural. When this was addressed in therapy, he stated that he chose to behave in these childish ways, even though he recognized they led to negative repercussions. Through further processing, he appeared to not have the maturity and social skills to engage peers or family members with more age-appropriate behavior. His behaviors set him up for rejection. He was hurt by peer mocking and non-acceptance. He felt he did not deserve the consequences of his behavior yet wanted to be socially connected. Unfortunately, his actions violate all three of the above considerations. He was having a negative impact on others, he acted outside of social norms, and he presented as odd or even selfish. The goal was to help this client "read his audience" and make logical choices to create better social acceptance without changing his identity.

It is important to be conscious of the Self and to weigh the considerations listed above. Being aware of the Core Self and acting on Core Self impulses are two separate things, and they can always be explored and assessed for open expression. Even though free and honest displays of emotion might have been more acceptable at our earlier stages of life, the current practice of totally expressing our Core Self can sometimes come across as selfish, immature, or overwhelming to others. To some it may seem as though certain limits are pushed to a level infringing on others' rights. However, an individual decision can be made about how and when a personal view or emotional response is presented.

Through this process, it is important to maintain an internal understanding of our Real Self while also being cognizant of what is regarded as good social practice of judgment. There is doubtfully very little if any constructive value in expressing negative or hurtful ideas that may predictably impact others. This might be seen in a situation when a person is asked a question of individual taste. A personal view may be an honest presentation of the Self, but it is based on an opinion. Recognizing the point of giving feedback is not always meant to be a criticism or critique. Rather it is more of an opportunity to share a subjective response. For example, if you attend your friend's art show at a gallery, your feedback may not be expected to be an assessment of the art. It is more of a personal and emotional response that may be more appropriate for that situation.

In various circumstances, withholding certain thoughts or feelings may actually be more reasonable than Honest Self sharing, as long as we are not compromising our personal values and beliefs. As they say, "timing is everything" and "know your audience." However, if there is an important and rational need to share a thought or feeling not aligned with another individual or group mentality, Honest Self expression may be necessary, as it is in line with your Core Self.

Behavioral Change

Just as it is good to be aware of the impact of our communications toward others, so too should we recognize that others may also want to communicate openly and effectively as their Core Self. While we likely accept others' positive traits and intentions, we will also likely react to their negative traits. These traits could include values, attitudes, opinions, and behaviors.

Though we recognize and might oppose the negative, we cannot expect others to alter their behavior due to our personal reaction. Should they choose to work on making individualized alterations and have some level of concern for others, change might actually occur. It may come through an awakening or genuine empathy for yourself and others. Here, the person would have to be internally motivated to make a personal change with how they express their negative traits.

In other circumstances, behavioral interventions can be used effectively toward personal change. This may be achieved in psychotherapy. The primary determinant of success comes when there is a genuine desire by a client to want to change, otherwise all the efforts toward a successful outcome will fail. This is true for any individual who wants to make a change in their life. Whether it is to increase a desired behavior or to decrease an unhealthy one, the behavioral approach has its place for useful therapeutic interventions.

Behavioral approaches are also commonly utilized by parents who apply them to raise children, as well as teachers when managing students and supervisors when motivating their employees. We even apply these techniques when wanting to change the behaviors of those we are close to, such as a friend or a social acquaintance. This type of shaping occurs regardless of whether it is being intentionally planned or as a subconscious attempt to edit another person's behavior.

Positive and negative reinforcement shape another person's actions through simple gestures or behaviors that can include verbal praise/criticism or particular consequences that will motivate a person to maintain or change a certain behavior. Even nonverbal metacommunications can edit another's behavior, such as communicating through physical gestures, facial expressions, or through the tone and amplitude of our speech. As human beings, we are constantly communicating to one another by way of direct and indirect messages that go beyond basic verbal messages. In the words of the Communications and Family Theorist Paul Watzlawick, "One cannot not communicate."

We are complex in the ways we convey messages to others due to the several levels of communication that occur. The hope is that we are consistent with our communication and congruent with the levels of messages that are simultaneously expressed. Not all individuals will respond to behavioral transactions. As previously discussed, a motivated person who wants to make a change is more likely to accept behavioral interventions prescribed by a therapist or counselor. If they are resistant to change, there will not be change. If they do not accept the benefits of change, there will not be change. Therefore, if a person carries a particular negative trait or possesses a nature that creates social problems for that individual, they might still maintain the behavior, unless they knowingly desire conscious change.

An example of this relates to Bradley, a fifteen-year-old client who shared his frustration regarding the behavior of an older sibling who constantly provoked him. The sibling made hurtful statements and "put-downs" while frequently boasting about his own life and his "amazing" accomplishments. Bradley stated that he chose to not respond to his sibling's unwarranted mistreatment as a means of minimizing the negative behavior. He believed his sibling wanted to irritate him and that if he showed his feelings of anger or hurt, he would be reinforcing his sibling's behavior to ultimately continue his pattern of annoyances. Most people, after receiving a silent response or unemotional feedback, will eventually ease up and quit their provocative but seemingly ineffective behavior.

The expected "reward" from purposely aggravating and making critical jabs toward his younger sibling should be surely lost due to Bradley's non-reaction. Provoking Bradley was not rewarding. It was predicted that the sibling would lose interest and eventually stop their actions due to the unanticipated lack of response by Bradley. Unfortunately, this was not the result. The nonreaction and repeated distancing by Bradley did not change his sibling's negative communication. The sibling seemed oblivious to the cold, aloof reaction Bradley portrayed. Instead, the sibling's bothersome behavior seemed to be more related to his own inherent negative traits of aggressiveness, thoughtlessness, arrogance, and conceitedness.

The question to consider from the above scenario: Why is it that we believe we can change or positively influence someone's negative behavior when it might be their true nature? Bradley gave no reaction to his sibling's negative communication, which was a simple behavioral shaping technique that should have been nonrewarding, yet the behavior continued. This might imply that while certain behaviors of an individual can be shaped, traits do not completely change because they are within a person's internal nature. Behavioral interventions may be less predictable when they are tied to a person's Core Self.

We are often well intentioned and hopeful when trying to help alter certain behaviors of another. Success may be achieved when that other person sees benefits to personal change and when they are motivated. It seems less likely to occur when the source of one's behavior originates from negative traits. It is also unlikely to occur when the reward for change feels minimal or the penalty seems insignificant. Everyone responds differently to consequences, whether positive or negative. It is more related to the person's nature, and they might not respond predictably to simple shaping.

Nonrewarding shaping (punishment or negative consequences) attempts may still result in the same continued behavior, but this depends on the individual. This might imply that certain traits of some people cannot be shaped since they are strongly set in their nature. If this is the case, it may be more beneficial to honestly share thoughts and feelings directly to that person. This is ideally done when the issue is important and emotionally safe to disclose. Maybe through this disclosure, the person will recognize that their behavior is an issue for you and might possibly affect others. The likelihood that this person will want to change behaviors needs to come from within, through personal choice.

Addressing Negativity

As individuals, we also want to overcome the weight of negative outside energies. They can ultimately influence our mood, thus affecting our general sense of well-being. Though we want to avoid any associated bad feelings, we may also try to change or adapt ourselves to the discomfort that was created, in order to best manage the negative surroundings. This is meant to minimize the uneasiness felt when we are unable to avoid the situation.

Knowing that there is inevitably going to be some form of negativity surrounding us at times, we can prepare for it and not feed into it. There can simply be a realistic awareness that we will encounter some level of negativity and not elevate it to a degree of such importance and negative impact. If we are to look around and focus on the incredible amount of support and positivity that actually does surround us, we will likely feel more alert, aware, and alive rather than hurt, overwhelmed, and cynical.

Human beings tend to be more influenced by negative experiences than positive ones. Studies have explored this phenomenon showing our propensity to overfocus on negative feelings related to our social interactions and other daily communications. There appears to be an underlying belief that with negativity, emotional harm might come to us. This Negativity Bias references our tendency to internalize negativity but also discount positive events or feelings. It is a cognitive bias acknowledging that when we experience both negative and positive events, or when surrounded by negative and positive people, uncomfortable feelings of a negative nature will tend to be the stronger element encountered. We may focus more on unpleasant material that carries significant weight in the direction of negativity, keeping us vigilant and alert. If we mostly experience positivity, we would instead feel more at peace.

Several of us may get stuck and dwell on negative conditions rather than the positive ones because negative experiences can feel so overwhelming to us. Let us consider a hypothetical situation where there is perhaps a 90 percent positive vibe surrounding an individual within a group setting (meaning 90 percent of the people there are kind, encouraging, and have positive intentions); 10 percent may then be considered negative. Even with this level of an outweighed positive imbalance, we tend to be hyperaware of the negative aspects of a situation and can feel overwhelmed by them. At times we might perseverate on the negative, which can drop our mood to a place of sadness, anxiety, and skepticism.

We feel bad when confronted with negativity. Even if it is infrequently present, it will eventually reveal itself as something heavier and much more pronounced than the positive that surrounds us. Positive vibes may be more present, but they are often "taken for granted." Positive vibes may be assumed to be normal and are even ignored by us, perhaps because of their higher frequency. The level of intensity for negative vibes frequently outweighs that of positive ones.

For some of us, difficult times may be remembered over the favorable times. Good experiences essentially lack discomfort, can feel temporary, and they seem to pass. Positive moments can be disregarded or undervalued and sometimes cannot compete with the negative moments, as small as they might be. In some situations, one negative statement can appear to wipe out a wide range of positive ones. An example of such an occurrence came from a client who shared about a miserable experience she encountered at her school PTA meeting.

Within the group of parents, the client held an office of moderate responsibility. She was well liked by the majority of the PTA members and was respected for her ideas and decision making. During one meeting, she shared such an idea for an event that seemed to excite fellow members and appeared to be overwhelmingly supported. Following the meeting, an unhappy group member, who had been silent during the meeting, began talking with others critically and disagreeably regarding the idea. This person seemed to carry some clout and wanted to influence others by dismissing the client's proposed idea. This was done outside the meeting. It was eventually shared with the client by various PTA members at a later date. The new communication by the group seemed to be that my client's idea and input was no longer valued or wanted.

In therapy, the client shared feelings of hurt and deception. Why were some of her peers against her, and why did some change their support of her proposal? She was receiving calls that her idea might need to be dropped and that the group should move on to some routine and unoriginal plans that were proposed in the past. The client had felt free to share a creative suggestion, and she was initially supported. After hearing about the source of the change, as well as experiencing a push to let go of her idea, the client no longer wanted to pursue it. The negative reaction felt too overwhelming for her, and she felt uncomfortable continuing. The client was affected by negative feedback and ridicule for being her Honest Self in a public forum. The impact of this negativity from a small minority was large. A single negative action went a long way.

In therapy, the client was asked to view her proposed idea from an objective place. She was encouraged to examine whether her idea actually had value and if she presented it in a direct and open way. She was clear that her presentation was shared as her Core Self and with honest expression. She further recognized that a significant acceptance was given by the group majority, and she could also acknowledge that the initial supporters were probably still in favor of her idea. She was then asked to imagine the people present at the next PTA meeting. She visualized those who would positively support her versus those who might be negative or opposed. She could see a room full of support with the exception of a few who would take a position against her. This approach helped center the client with renewed confidence once she realized that her cognitive distortions were preventing her from accepting the higher levels of positive support over the relatively minimal negative criticism.

The client's comfort grew, and she acknowledged that her presentation was a genuine, caring approach to help the success of the PTA. Even though her idea and her Core Self identity were not fully accepted by a limited few, there was enough support for her to continue what she had started. She was aware that the majority of her peers were still in favor of her idea. Also, on a deeper level, she did not need to feel intimidated nor have to edit what she wanted to propose.

Initially, the negative feedback felt so intense and overwhelming that the client nearly abandoned her original idea. This would have been due to a small ring of individuals who tried to covertly snatch control of a positively functioning situation. This negative faction seemed to want power. They also seemed to struggle with the creativity of the client. Had they truly felt the idea was not in the best interest of the group, they could have addressed it openly during the initial meeting and shared their concerns.

The interesting side to this story is how common this same scenario gets played out in different settings. I am aware of how children and adolescents must often handle bullies in their schoolyard who want things done their way. There is also that uncomfortable feeling experienced when receiving negative feedback as a consequence for expressing individuality. It occurs in work settings and volunteer organizations where there is competition as well as issues of leadership, with the risk of becoming Lost. The negative feedback is presented in both verbal and nonverbal forms.

Feelings of disapproval or rejection may be experienced and may prevent a person from pursuing creative ideas that could cause others to feel threatened. This arises even within large extended family systems where someone wants to claim power through either overt or subtle ways. These are all similar processes with manipulations for personal gain and with little regard for personal and individualistic styles that do not match up with the edict of the moment.

What to Do

Ultimately, the ideal interactions between people are those that are supportive and encouraging. However, some individuals do not aspire toward greater understanding and better communication skills. Why not "raise the bar" to improve oneself? Perhaps for some, they may resort to a form of defensiveness when feeling low self-esteem. They could certainly benefit themselves and others by putting forth the effort to improve social interactions by aiding those who struggle and motivating others to do their best. Instead, the energy may shift to bring others down. They may direct their efforts more toward making others feel inferior when they do not believe they themselves can grow. As a result, they may hurt, humiliate, or insult others due to their own insecurities. They can seem to be critical of others rather than striving to build their own self-esteem. Sometimes this feels easier than working on oneself and developing a better self-image.

Therefore, striving to understand the workings of our inner Core Self is important. With a deeper knowledge of our coping mechanisms in times of stress, along with self-acceptance, a person is better equipped to be more able to accept others for who they are without hurting self-esteem for either self or others. Positive connections may be made with some individuals due to high levels of comfort from a shared compatibility. Having a mutual understanding with reciprocated acceptance makes social interactions enjoyable.

Recognizing differences with some people can also be valued. It helps us to choose our level of openness and to make decisions over interacting as a Real or Honest Self. Not all social exchanges require judgments of one's level of openness, but it helps to manage our internal struggles when presented with negative individuals and negative situations. We can make choices about whom we want to interact with and at what level to present ourselves. As long as we do not resort to escaping into a Lost Self state, we are more aligned with who we are and what approach we will have with others.

Both negative and positive Core Self traits exist for each person. Perhaps the only way for a person to change and redevelop an unwanted negative trait is from within, by choice. The person must recognize that certain negative traits and associated behaviors can cause relational problems with others. If they are willing to accept this premise and sincerely want better relationships, there are healthy cognitive and behavioral changes that can be chosen. This type of transformation is qualitatively different from a person whose Core Self is edited when shaped by a group.

Through group shaping, a person might experience pressure to change their belief system and to behave inconsistently with their own true nature. Becoming aware of one's own thoughts, feelings, and behavior and their impact on others allows for making self-change that has a personal purpose. A successful outcome occurs when such insight accompanies the desire for positive individual change and social interest.

Chapter 6

Acceptance and Human Variability (Acceptance of Self and Others)

What I am is good enough if I would only be it openly.

—Carl Rogers

We are all unique human beings. The unlimited variations among us are what make people individuals. We are born with a specific temperament that is observable from our early development and continues within our Core Self. No one completely looks, thinks, or acts exactly like another, though similarities may exist. Even if we try our best to mimic and reproduce someone else's look and style, we will ultimately exhibit true parts of ourselves. It is impossible to accurately match another person with exact precision. There is too much trait variability, and it is all influenced by personal temperament. We are all different, and our exact trait combinations cannot be fully experienced by another.

There is such diversity among humans. Collectively, we have a multitude of characteristics that present as infinite combinations, with varying levels of intensity. These variations may be seen in one's cognitive abilities, personality traits, physical appearance, and social skills. Other more obvious differences are recognizable through a person's age, gender, race, and cultural background. Beyond these examples, traits of the self may also be influenced by the environment and personal social experiences. Through these variables, it is therefore important to emphasize the value of each individual as someone who is unique and special. It is healthy to accept one's own self and embrace the individuality of what is ultimately one's Core Self.

Joining Others While Staying in the Real Self

It is good to be unique. Sometimes we might struggle to share a thought or an idea that has originality, since it may actually be separate from standards that are more commonly supported by others. This is especially true when a majority has already decided on what is acceptable, and there is a consistent approval and embracement that gets maintained without challenge. As adults, we likely experience this tendency socially, in the workplace or in other settings and situations. There may be expectations to comply with general procedures or directives. Here, maintaining one's own uniqueness is challenging and might not match the standards one might have chosen independently. In some circumstances it may be appropriate to join the majority through compromise and in the name of cooperation. The Real Self can still be maintained as long as personal values are not compromised.

Oftentimes children and adolescents experience peer pressure to accept a group's mentality. Examples of this can be seen through a young person's physical presentation, such as how they dress, what brand of clothing they wear, hairstyle, and even how they express themself. On another level, there may also be values that are compromised or judgments made about others that represent a group opinion and not an individual's. This is challenging when certain values are meaningful and represent different principles or morals from the group.

Sometimes differing group values may not be so distressing. A person might accept the dissimilarity when their aim is to join the group. In such situations, an individual may compromise what they actually prefer simply to "fit in" with the group. An example might be a child who is affiliating with a group of peers who value sports. The peers talk about professional athletes, they know their stats, collect trading cards, and play sports activities during recess, lunch, and after school. Should one choose to enter this group, there is a likelihood that peer acceptance will involve participation in sports.

What if the child has little interest in sports but really likes some of the peers in this group? The child will likely struggle to fully connect unless they accept themself and know their own limits of this social engagement. It might be more reasonable for this child to develop separate one-on-one friendships with some of the group's peers rather than try to join an uncomfortable group mentality. As discussed in the adult example, a Real Self presentation may continue if personal values and interests are not compromised.

Sometimes we might withhold creative thoughts or ideas when they differ from views that are recurrently supported by others. This is common when a majority determines what is acceptable, and their opinion is consistently supported without opposition. Even the most diplomatic or persuasive approaches may not engage others enough for them to become interested or to consider acceptance of a new idea. There may be a risk of alienation should someone choose an outside presentation of individuality. These dilemmas will happen when we want to join with others while still wanting to maintain our individuality. Personally, I can recall several instances of having this struggle.

On Being a Unique Individual

I recognize that my desire to be unique and different from others goes back to an early age. I have clear recollections of wanting to stand out or separate from others, based on my own individuality. I became frustrated if I perceived that others tried to imitate me or attempted what I construed as borrowing my ideas. I was not grandiose about my areas of uniqueness; I felt I was quite average in my physical presentation, athletic abilities, and interest in classroom learning activities. I just wanted to see myself as a separate person within my peer group.

I was not envious of others who had their own special skills, but I did experience childhood jealousies (such as wanting a toy like another child had or going somewhere fun and special as another might have experienced). Instead I was more impressed and supportive of other people's unique abilities and ideas. For myself, I wanted to be who I am; from others, I wanted to be appreciated for being myself. I was fortunate enough to want individuality at an early age. I was too young and probably oblivious of the potential peers teasing me for being different. These challenges of individuality came a little later in life.

I remember being a five-year-old child in my kindergarten class. The students were given drawing materials with instructions to draw and color what we created. At that age, I was somewhat ambidextrous, always using my left and right hands equally for different tasks. That particular day, I was switching back and forth with my writing utensils. When my left hand was tiring, I changed over and wrote with my other hand. Miss P—came to my group table and questioned my use of two hands instead of just one like the other children. At that time I felt pressured to make a hand-use commitment. I chose to use the hand that was different from my peers at the table. I recall the moment of consciously choosing to use my left hand. Though ambidextrous, I was happy to show off my identity as a lefty. To this day, I write and throw with my left hand; however, I can choose to use either hand with many other activities.

I suppose at age five my choice to be left handed could be considered oppositional or attention seeking. This may be valid, but the moment sticks in my mind as an opportunity to be separate from the group. Though my choice was to possess an uncommon behavior, it was also a fun and exciting opportunity to own this characteristic with its uniqueness, since it was not directly affecting others. I did not risk group rejection or peer ridicule. I was simply known by my teacher and the peers at my table as the kid who uses his left hand. Little did I know that I was not alone as a lefty. I eventually realized that I was not as unique as I thought, and I was surprised to learn of others with my same hand preference. This turned out to feel somewhat positive, considering only 10 percent of the population is left handed, a small, unique group of us.

A couple of years later, I was signed up for Pee Wee T-Ball. I was the only left hander on the team. From this, one of my coaches nicknamed me "Wrong Armed." I think some kids would have felt embarrassed with this label, however I actually appreciated the nickname as it somehow highlighted a unique ability of my own. I certainly needed this, considering my athletic skills were somewhat average. Unfortunately, my Wrong Armed nickname changed midseason after my mother accidentally bleached my dark blue Mets team jersey. My nickname changed to "The Guy with the Bleached Shirt."

What is significant is how I wanted to hold a position of individuality. It was not opposition or defiance that motivated me, but rather a goal of being unique or different. I did not choose to be outrageous or seek attention. My purpose was to feel personally grounded in who I am. This was an important theme that I encountered for a significant period in my life.

I always appreciated being given a compliment or side observation from another person commenting on my level of individuality, uniqueness, and sometimes creativity. The old saying "think outside the box" was a personal motto of mine that still drives my energies today. I wanted to be defined as an original and not one who subscribes to the way things are routinely done. I also found that I had developed a manner of counteraction by trying to avoid copying or duplicating other people's ideas.

I believe my draw toward individuality came from both Core Self traits as well as learned behaviors. I realize there were several creative individuals that impressed and influenced me during my early years. I recognized their own uniqueness coupled with their confidence. I modeled the concept of their originality, which led me to feel empowered to speak up and present my own individuality.

Recognizing there was a social side to my drive for individuality, there were genetic factors that also contributed. Certain personal traits were likely passed down from family members who each showed some level of their individuality. Putting these elements together, they add up to the conceptual world of "who I am" and "how I behave." I am not fully aware of the extent to which I behaved with uninhibited individuality before the age of five, but I observe that most children of this age group express themselves without major guardedness. They commonly show a freedom that is self-focused but may also be hidden when they are afraid of a negative outcome.

Prior to age five, did I feel safe expressing myself as I truly felt in the moment, unafraid of potential consequences? Was I able to laugh or cry without self-editing? Did I play freely, while exploring the things that felt fun or important as a toddler? These are interesting considerations for those early years.

As a young child, I appreciated my individuality. I do, however, recall facing repercussions for outspoken behaviors during middle childhood through adolescence, whether at home or in school. I was not rebellious, but I was occasionally open and candid with my impression of things. Negative reactions from authority figures or peers could sometimes shut me down.

Following my time of uninhibited openness, I tended to minimize unique parts of myself due to anticipated unsupportive responses. Since there were consistent outcomes that felt emotionally hurtful, I managed to keep much of my drive for individuality subtle and less apparent to those with whom I had regular interactions. I had moved from being an Honest Self type to a sometimes Real or Hidden Self.

As a Real Self, I could remain conscious of my inner thoughts and feelings, yet make a decision to not share them openly. As a Hidden Self, I was more likely to deny the unique parts of myself. The problem with the Hidden Self mentality was that I was not feeling comfortably safe being myself. Fitting in felt more secure. Much of my creative side was then pushed aside, and cooperative behaviors became more routine. Opportunities to share unique and personal thoughts could raise my anxiety and, at times, induce panic reactions.

The theme of wanting to show my uniqueness existed since childhood and still continues today. Along the way, the thoughts of claiming my own self-identity have remained, but the personal struggle for acceptance and how to fit in socially has oftentimes been difficult. Growing up, there were many times while striving to match the group that I felt out of sync and alone. I am aware of others who relate to these struggles since their goal was not to be an outsider but rather to feel acceptance by the group.

When making a personal decision to embrace individuality, there may be risks of rejection, taunting, or mockery. It is here that personal self-acceptance can prompt one to still be real with openness and to improve confidence. At times, others might try to create feelings of embarrassment for you, since you have allowed the Self to be congruent (who you are) within different social contexts. These uncomfortable moments can help motivate a person to be stronger with the Self, while others may still feel apprehensive. However, the more comfortable we can behave as our own true nature, the less likely we will feel the anxiety or depression associated with incongruity.

Mutual Acceptance

Recognition of the Core Self within one's self and others is a critical part of positive interactions that embrace individuality. Shared or complementary support among individuals creates welcoming mutual understandings and promotes acceptance. We do not necessarily need to be in agreement with another person's viewpoint, but by accepting their perspective without criticism or judgment, we provide validation and support.

Reciprocal acknowledgment between individuals helps build healthy relationships. From this, we gain the ability to convey acceptance of others. We also want to feel unconditionally welcomed by others and recognized for who we are. This helps us to feel comfortable being ourselves. Ultimately, we should simultaneously feel the freedom to pursue personal interests as well as have comfort in expressing our personal opinions. We should never feel as if we must change ourselves to please others, just as we should not try to change others to match ourselves.

Imagination and inventiveness are components of originality. They may become more accessible as the individual reclaims the elements of their Core Self. Allowing ourselves to experience such creativity expands our freedom of expression, which can definitely increase our sense of well-being. Unfortunately, some people may become unsupportive and even critical of another's originality. This can feel especially sensitive when coming from a person whose opinion has meaning and value to you. Under these circumstances it is important to regard the disparity of views as what they really are: separate perspectives by two different people, both entitled to experience the same issues in different ways. Afterall, as much as we might seek acceptance, we might also want to show acceptance for the other person/people in this situation. The communication comes down to mutual respect for one another's individuality and unique creativity.

Some of us believe that creativity is meant to be primarily experienced through the arts, such as drawing, acting, singing, cooking, dancing, playing music, etc. However, creativity as a form of originality also relates to how we think, problem-solve, and interact with others socially. When negative past experiences cause us to question who we really are and may have shaped the way we interact with others, there will be a need to retrieve the unique qualities we once shared outwardly.

It is best when we can allow ourselves the freedom to revisit the person we have suppressed and to not hide our creative self. We can allow for real feelings to be felt and expressed. The more one overthinks and questions themself, the less likely they are able to feel and be their true Core Self.

Managing the Various Roles We Carry

We are challenged to be our Core Self within the several arenas where we live. We carry many roles combined with varying behaviors during the course of our lifetime. With each role, it is reasonable that we may maintain our Core Self yet still engage several groups or individuals differently. How we conduct ourselves often depends on who is present and what is to be communicated.

There is a responsibility to properly match the appropriate communication with the right audience. For instance, how does a parent effectively communicate to their child? It would not be appropriate for them to relate to their child the same way they might engage a friend or peer from work. However, the personal style of the individual might remain constant among different groups. The Core Self can still be present, only communicated in a better, relatable way.

Among the various roles we carry, we are likely to behave differently. This depends on the specific role presented, as well as the situation we are engaged in while communicating to a particular group or person. The Core Self should still be present and unchanged. Traits and temperament exist yet may be assembled in ways that correspond to the situation at hand. Certain life approaches such as "caring" and "emotional awareness" are examples of core traits that may stay consistent as threads that are woven into each of the multiple roles an individual carries in their life.

A "healthy" person will be able to maintain the characteristics of their Core Self into the varied roles carried within their lives. To some, the concept of uniqueness within our roles seems vague and abstract. However, Core Self characteristics may permeate the various roles and represent the true identity that exists within. We should expect certain self-elements to cross over as a presence within the roles we carry.

An example can be seen by an individual who possesses the above mentioned traits of "caring" and "emotional awareness." While in the parental role, these traits may be seen when they communicate with their child. They may also be evident when this person carries other roles, such as when they are interacting with coworkers, personal friends, or other family members. This is because their temperament is constant and should be present within the varied relationships they have.

For myself, there are several different roles I have carried within my life journey. Currently, I am a husband, father, son, grandfather, son-in-law, brother, brother-in-law, uncle, nephew, friend, volunteer, psychologist, supervisor, employee, coach, and several others. With each role I maintain a Real Self mentality, yet I often behave differently within each of my communication sets. In part this is due to the expectations and responsibilities of the particular role or position I carry. I am not necessarily wrong to behave differently with different people, when considering my various connections with each of them separately.

I can still be congruent as my Core Self while adapting and getting along with different people or groups. My behavior relates to the role I carry with that person or particular group. If I were to treat everyone connected to me in the same way, I would be out of touch with others. Instead, I try to be a realist and strive to adapt or get along with those I communicate with at any given time. Depending on the level of comfort I feel, this might determine whether I am engaged as a Real Self or an Honest Self.

Those who are unable to effectively adjust to others and their surroundings may be struggling emotionally. Sometimes a cycle occurs, placing a person in the recurrence of working to be one's Real Self yet feeling disconnected from the group. This is a person who wants to affiliate with the group yet recognizes there are significant differences in the way they approach life. They may have dissimilar interests and carry a different value system.

Within this cycle, one makes a decision of either pulling away or re-engaging with the group again. If one has low social skills and difficulty connecting to others, there may be an end result of nonacceptance from the group, which can feel discouraging. In this scenario negative reinforcements often trigger feelings of low self-esteem and symptoms of depression. Not knowing one's role or how one fits in may also increase a person's anxiousness. With these situations it may be reasonable to initially adapt to the group yet not compromise personal values. This helps a person stay somewhat engaged, without feeling overloaded or giving up parts of the Self.

Eventually, by working on the Core Self and developing a clearer and stronger self-knowledge, self-acceptance should increase and become less stressful. As long as a person is aware of their own thoughts and feelings, they will be moving in the right direction. Even if our actions and compliance with a group mentality seems incongruent with one's Core Self, we must realize the group is not what defines who we are. Under these conditions, it may feel acceptable to choose some level of affiliation with the group while still maintaining one's Core Self. When we are thinking as our Real or Honest Self, we are most self-aware. A positive self-acceptance of our internal awareness is the primary goal.

Masks We Wear

As we strive to know our Core Self, we may be influenced by our own masks that we wear publicly. We wear these masks to interact and meet the demands of society as well as to behave in ways that are appropriate and within social norms. Depending on the setting and the people present, we choose different masks to adapt to our surroundings. The issue of concern is that when we use our mask to conceal our Real Self, we may become a Lost Self who is not consciously aware of our true nature.

When we overidentify with a mask, we may lose sight of our real identity. As a Lost Self, there is a lack of internal awareness and only an effort to fit in. As a Hidden Self, a person is aware of their mask and their accompanying performance but still chooses to conceal who they are. With this Hidden Self state, the individual is aware that they are actually not genuine with how they appear to others, but they wear the mask for social acceptance and may consciously give up personal values during this process.

An important distinction between the Hidden and Lost Self is that the Lost Self has little to no insight regarding their interpersonal identity. This person views themself as someone needing to fit in but shows no drive to establish the differences between Self and others. They may simply define themself by such things as gender, religion, job, and socioeconomic status or acknowledge roles like mother, sister, wife, friend, or employee, each carrying a different set of identity characteristics but with more of a stereotypical version of the role. They do not separate from the clichéd or conventional version of the identities. They are simply "mother" when it is time to assert that identification, and they try to fit into the mold that demonstrates the title. Since universal or archetypal images exist of what the mother is, it is not hard to exemplify the features of the character.

Similarities exist between the Hidden Self and the concept of the persona. The archetype of the persona was introduced by Swiss psychiatrist Carl Jung as a concept to explain the different social masks we wear publicly. Depending on the social context, the persona is that part of us that tries to assimilate within certain groups or situations in order to protect us from negative reactions and feedback. The persona may aid us to fit in with social norms and helps us control primitive feelings and impulses that are not socially acceptable. With this persona archetype, one can try to better adapt to social groups, as well as society in general, while not fully revealing who they truly are.

A young girl entering a social group of girls for the first time may present a persona that matches the image of being cool and aloof. However a more honest portrayal of herself would be a bright and happy girl who feels anxious in new social situations. The same may be seen for a new manager joining a company. The manager presents themself as serious with a strong work ethic, when in reality they are actually playful and easygoing. Both of these examples demonstrate individuals who mask their true nature in order to match the role that they want to present socially.

According to Jung, the persona forms in early childhood as a means of helping us follow norms or expectations from parents, other authority figures, and peers. Through the adaptation portrayed by the persona, certain conduct and characteristics are learned as socially acceptable and may continue. Conversely, other behaviors and self-features may not be seen as desirable and can result in the receipt of negative feedback or rejection. Through this process, the persona offers us a safe way to interact socially with a type of guardedness that helps us get along with others. Though safe, this person may still feel incongruent with their Core Self.

Interestingly, the masks we wear are not solely displayed to others in person but also through shared presentations such as websites and online applications. These social networking introductions appear less personal yet can create an image of a person that is unclear or inaccurate. Prior to social media, we portrayed the different versions of ourselves through a physical presence and spoken language. Presently, much of our communication is through email, texts, and various social media platforms.

In some ways these communication changes have complicated how we present ourselves socially. It can take some individuals further away from their Real or Honest Self, if they are actively attempting to present as someone they are not. For some individuals, social media has increased the option of lying, which puts us closer to behaving as Lost or Hidden Selves. Much of the motivation to do this comes from the false images competitively shared by others. This can lead both children and adults into entering a cycle of competition or keeping up to fit in.

The concept of not fitting in has also become more complex. Social interactions that occur live and in person may allow separate time for an individual to process and debrief feelings following uncomfortable exchanges. When an individual is provoked in person, they have options on how to respond. The outcome may result in verbal arguments or other negative exchanges. However, depending on the situation, there may be alternative choices in handling the matter. Sometimes the problem goes away; other times it continues, but there are options for other social interventions when the issue persists.

With social media, negative exchanges may feel never ending since often what is written never goes away, and it may reach a person even when they are physically removed from a bad situation. Cyberspace is omnipresent and hard to avoid. Cyberbullies share similarities to the bullies of the playground, and their intent is to be hurtful. Social inclusion or exclusion among groups provokes the victims with a message of possible rejection and not being accepted. It negatively influences those who are involved to play along or get hurt by certain communities in cyberspace. This form of social engagement definitely challenges us in our pursuit of self-acceptance and in being our Real Self.

We are often placed in situations requiring us to choose between being true to our Core Self or fitting in unnaturally. It is a blessing when our Core Self matches the group value, but this is not always the case. At face value, the choice seems simple. Choosing to be one's Core Self in a social situation merely requires us to be ourselves without acting false. All that is required of us is to be genuine.

With such a clear-cut choice, we are likely to believe in a positive return from a presentation of openness and honesty. Even if our Core Self choice is not aligned with the popular beliefs of the group, shouldn't one be credited for their uniqueness and freedom to express a different thought? However, the bigger question that usually floats in one's mind is, Would I rather be a follower and feel accepted, or would I rather be myself and risk rejection?

Support or Criticism for Uniqueness

There is a fortunate group of people who admire individuality and get mental stimulation from unique and creative thinking. Though this group may work on their own individuality, they also encourage and support others to do the same. In such situations, a person might be respected for having alternative views when the group mentality rewards openness of thought. Yet another common reaction may cause discomfort from criticism. There may be a tendency for the group to ignore or squelch the presentation of the outlier who ventures to think independently at the risk of group alienation. Sometimes that question of choosing between an Honest Self or an adaptable, malleable person who is simply fitting in is more complex, yet it is often self-answered within a quick second. Here, we are forced to weigh the choices.

Through swift calculations, we can decipher the costs and gains between unedited self-honesty versus cooperative acceptance of a group mentality. Should one decide to be themself, the reward of self-congruence is appealing since it is self-acceptance and not acting in a way that takes away from one's personal identity. The person may be at peace with themself. They are true to themself without feeling forced to comply with an ideology opposed to their belief system.

The cost, however, may be rejection from the group. This may be a momentary experience that is semitolerable, or it may set the stage for deeper alienation that places this person, who has honest integrity, to be judged as odd or different and have their opinions discounted. The alternative is to cooperate with the group mentality. Sometimes this is uncomfortable, especially when values are an issue. Other times cooperation is superficial and not taken very seriously. It can simply be a means of just getting along, nothing more.

I had a young college student ask me a question about maintaining her Real Self while striving to fit in and feel acceptance among female peers in a school organization. The group of girls was somewhat established due to several students returning from the previous year. This student often felt left out, dismissed, and uninvited to peer group outings/activities that were technically separate from the group's school events. The student admitted feeling hurt and rejected, and sought to understand if there was a purpose in her being left out. The student wondered if she did something offensive, which further fed into her own low self-image. The student also questioned whether there were some personal issues operating, yet she was aware of other similar girls who were solidly accepted within this group.

At this early stage of therapy, the student and I examined the situation, exploring the student's own actions within the group as well as seeing if any former themes were reoccurring from previous group affiliations. We determined she has felt displaced within other peer groups in the past. Presenting as her Honest Self did not always help build relationships with peers during times of initial group introductions. She frequently felt alienated. Her typical response to feeling rejected was to act out in ways that were confrontational and usually left her feeling hurt and angry. However this time, she acknowledged her sad feelings, which was sincerely truthful.

The student showed growth through self-understanding with her deeper feelings. Her question of how to maintain her Real Self in this situation was a genuine desire to work on social skills while not giving up her identity. She chose to work on becoming more sociable and verbal in group situations. She also made the effort to be less isolated and more active within the group dynamics. Lastly, she realized that she did not have to work so hard to feel acceptance from the whole group and that a few improved relationships would be rewarding.

Her hope was to maintain her Real Self while feeling connected and accepted by her peer group. The student did not want to give up the parts of herself that she valued and made up the core of her identity. The process of treatment went on to explore the meaning of assimilation while not giving up personal values. There was a wish to feel acceptance from the group. This could occur safely as long as the student maintained her Real Self while recognizing that assimilation was alright and that she did not have to give up her Core Self identity.

The process of assimilation includes trying to understand and connect with something in common. It is an activity where someone joins others to be similar and together. We see people try to assimilate on a basic level when they are new to an established group or organization. On a larger scale, we see it when foreigners try to be part of a new culture.

I am aware of my grandparents' movement toward assimilation on an even deeper level. They managed to survive the Armenian Genocide and eventually left their country following World War I. Their journey ended in Mexico City. They were immigrants with no family and with very limited money. My grandparents spoke Armenian, Turkish, and Kurdish fluently but now had to learn the Spanish language in addition to learning Mexican culture.

My grandfather was a shoemaker from the Old Country. He began demonstrating his trade publicly on the streets so potential customers would recognize his skills with repairing and making shoes. He was successful at his trade, and the family eventually did well in their new country. This was the beginning of my family's movement from survival to cultural assimilation.

Though my grandparents could socially engage with other Armenians living in Mexico, they all entered the new culture with open minds, understanding the benefits of assimilation rather than isolation. They still maintained their values and unique types of behavior and thought. They preserved their Armenian heritage through such things as language, food, church, and leisure interests, but they also learned Spanish, cooked Mexican dishes, and engaged in social activities associated with Mexican culture. They learned to connect with others while not abandoning their own identity.

Starting a new life in a new land without the support of family members was extremely difficult. The family, especially my grandfather, understood the necessity of moving past a place of emotional safety (his Armenian culture) into a place of engagement with the people he began to interact with. They chose to develop new relationships and aided their children with becoming part of Mexican society. They accepted their new culture rather than resisted it. They also maintained important parts of their own heritage and never let go of them. Some of those parts of my ancestry were passed on to me and now to my children.

This brief example of cultural assimilation is shared as a means of recognizing the value of cooperation and collaboration within an established system. A person may maintain certain aspects of the Self, whether as personal morals, social values, or cultural background, yet still manage to "get along" within a group or system that is different from what they are accustomed to experiencing.

My grandparents did not have to give up parts of the Self or minimize the comfort felt from their own culture of origin. They benefited from open-mindedness and developed new communication with others that supported mutual acceptance. My grandparents understood the importance of joining with other individuals and connecting to their community as they still kept true to their own identity.

Ultimately, it is good to be our Real Self. Honest Self engagement may also feel good; it's a matter of comfort in revealing parts of the Core Self. Occasionally, we might grapple with sharing personal thoughts and feelings, especially if they create obvious differences between ourselves and the majority. Sometimes our beliefs and values are dissimilar from the standards that are supported by others. In these situations we can still be aware of differences while maintaining our own unique identities.

Though there may be a possibility of distancing ourselves from others by choosing an outside presentation of individuality, it is our choice. These difficulties may occur when we desire to join others while still wanting to maintain our Real Self. We have such human variability that we cannot expect to all think, feel, and behave in the same way. The optimal goal is for us to have self-acceptance. Through this, we may experience mutual acceptance from others and similar acceptance toward them.

Chapter 7

Distancing from the Self
(Core Self Denial)

You will either step forward into growth,
or you will step backward into safety.

—Abraham Maslow

There are different ways of understanding a person's history of moving away from their Core Self. Sometimes it arises in the early stages of a person's life and persists as a safe way to get along with others. Other times it happens during specific circumstances with possible recurrences. Regardless of the timing, the shift from being our Core Self to distancing from the Self can be examined with insight and self-acceptance.

Generally, a shift may occur as a means of trying to cooperate with social norms and fitting in with group expectations. Sometimes it happens as an avoidance of negative consequences. Other times a denial of Self comes from a personal desire to feel part of the bigger and more acceptable group that may also seem more favored or admired. Regardless of the motivation, conscious and subconscious processes are occurring. Through either process, the person is pulled away from the core of being themself. At some level, they likely have concerns about individual and group rejections.

Conscious and Subconscious Processes

The two processes examined here are our conscious and subconscious mind. We are conscious when we are aware of ourselves and the world around us. On a more significant level, conscious awareness may relate to personal insights, such as "this is why I feel this way" or "I react to this because of that." It is part of understanding thoughts and feelings as well as our actions.

With conscious awareness, our choices may be better understood, such as acting in a certain way to fit in or behaving in a manner expected by others to better match a situation.

The subconscious mind is deeper and not fully recognized by the individual. It too affects thoughts, feelings, and actions, though it is mostly out of a person's awareness. We are not fully aware of this part of our mind, yet it strongly influences us. Knowing the Self through the subconscious is accessible if pursued and processed correctly. It can help a person gain useful insights and self-understanding as well as prompt openness for change.

Conscious and subconscious processing can be viewed as distinct functions of the mind that we each possess. An alternate view is that they can operate together as part of a continuum, beginning with a conscious act that eventually transforms to become subconscious over time. For instance, we may consciously start an action, such as guardedness or compliance, based on our insecurities or social discomfort. This might occur when feeling disconnected to a group with whom we would like to engage. Awareness of such a feeling can create anxiety.

Through conscious repetitive practice of trying to join the group (perhaps by stating things that sound acceptable), we might eventually rationalize that there are greater benefits through minimizing our individuality or denying our own unique differences from the group. Over time we may subconsciously operate as if we are more comfortable portraying ourselves with the group's mentality instead of our own. By behaving less like our Real Self, we are not evolving. Instead, we are regressing and subconsciously behaving as if our social engagement is natural. This is a source of self-incongruity, and it can increase the likelihood of depressive symptoms.

The unique operations of our conscious and subconscious mind are special functions that can also relate to each other. This may occur when certain conscious discomforts are actively avoided, and they are replaced by new thoughts, feelings, or actions that become so routine that they are expressed almost naturally. It is a shift from one level of awareness to another on a continuum. When routine behaviors are displayed almost mechanically, there may be deeper feelings of incongruity or a distancing of the Self that are out of our conscious awareness.

Conscious Acting	→	Repetitive Practices	→	Leads to Subconscious Acting
(Anxious Discomforts)				(Depressive Symptoms May Emerge)

When nonauthentic repetitive behavior occurs, we may experience symptoms of depression. This is because there is cognitive dissonance between conscious, unpleasing actions that are contrary to what the Real or Honest Self would do naturally. By the time a person moves on the continuum where they are operating subconsciously, the acting seems embedded in the presentation of the individual, and the Lost Self emerges almost naturally. Those acting consciously as a Hidden Self can appear to fit in social situations almost seamlessly and portray a person who is aligned with the groups they engage. Both of these Selves struggle emotionally, since their actions differ from their natural Core Self.

Typical illustrations of distance versus acceptance of one's Core Self may be seen through certain social roles we carry. These could include relationships with others through volunteer groups, religious organizations, or the work environment. Our interactions may be telling and help define whether we are actually more of our Core Self or someone who has strayed. Getting along with others may result in team efforts for the purpose of cooperation. Sometimes it is reasonable to get along with a group or organizational mentality, as long as it does not compromise personal values or beliefs.

There are occasions where one is uncomfortably participating socially yet feels an obligation to get along. This is still a form of cooperation, but the person is likely unhappy and feels disingenuous. At other times, a person is unaware that they are distant from their Core Self, and they go along with the group regardless of how they feel. The conscious or subconscious process of drifting from the Core Self can be a difficult experience, especially when one feels powerless in their operations and how they dissimulate while engaging others.

Adjusting to Fit In

Seeing how one "used to be" and "what they have become" are examples of recognizing that one learned to fit into a new community or group culture. Regarding work or job identities, though some have specifically chosen their path as it matches or compliments their Core Self, others work diligently to fit in as they struggle for acceptance and getting ahead. These individuals may feel disconnected to their work culture and may be less like their Core Self.

One example is the person who has worked in the same corporate environment for years. Such tenacious longevity can create a type of person who epitomizes their corporate culture. Unfortunately, some of these individuals experience discomfort and symptoms of dysphoria, since they have progressively developed an act that is outside their Real Self. They are acting as they should, to fit into a structure that pulls for an expected type of appropriateness. Such an appearance may occur even though it is not their personal choice. It may feel safer to be a Hidden Self rather than the Real Self.

When consciously aware as a Hidden Self, a person tries their best to portray an individual who others want to see. When done flawlessly, the act is welcomed and accepted. Originality and creativity from the individual may be missing, but concealing maintains the status quo and will not ruffle anyone's feathers. For instance, if an expert in their field is planning to lecture to a group of colleagues, they might explore the accepted protocol and style of presenting as it fits the expectations of the audience. Based on this, they might choose to avoid sharing personal viewpoints that may be innovative or controversial. A cautious approach might be to follow the topic with basic information and only cover facts with significant findings from known studies. The expert might feel it is best to only share what is expected and already known.

Such a bland presentation is safe but misses the uniqueness that is part of the person's thoughts and distinctive personality. The problem is that this limited behavior produces discomfort and feelings of frustration. If they choose to present as their Real or Honest Self, they may feel challenged or critically questioned. Sometimes it feels easier to fit the expectations of others since managing anxiety can feel more uncomfortable.

However, they can also present what they do know and not share personal knowledge that is cutting edge or unusual. This would be safe, but still trying to get to a place of comfort might be challenging. It is likely to be more demanding to present with a Real or Honest Self mentality, but it will allow for innovation and freedom for the individual. Though taxing, it is qualitatively different from the anxiety felt by the Hidden Self. It allows for more openness, yet the person runs the risk of rejection or being out of favor with the group.

Concealing the Self to Fit In

Constant Hidden Self behavior is very stressful. These people are cautiously acting and giving an appearance of being someone they are not. Social situations can feel uncomfortable. Hidden Self individuals are consciously aware of the deception they have created and conceal it from others. It becomes fragile, like a "house of cards" running the risk of collapse at any moment.

This individual intentionally strives to convince others that they are a particular person. They choose to follow a clear path of social acceptance and will not set themself up for outside criticism or ultimate rejection. The person's true identity is purposely withheld so they are not found out. Feelings of anxiety will be present since a person is not being their Real Self. Instead, they are hiding and only showing behaviors that are mostly not their own.

Similarities exist between the Real and Hidden Self. For example, each of these versions of the Self have some level of understanding of who they truly are. Also in common is that they are not obliged to reveal inner thoughts and feelings. They may keep personal thoughts and feelings to themselves but for different reasons. The label of being a Real or Hidden Self depends on what the individual's motivation is. What is their purpose?

If the goal is meant to conceal parts of the Self that do not match well enough to others, they are more of a Hidden Self. Such a person is essentially minimizing who they really are and acting in ways to gain the approval of others. The Real Self may also withhold inner thoughts and feelings but for other reasons. They may choose silence to avoid unnecessary conflict or refrain from sharing material that could negatively impact the feelings of a person or group. The Real Self knows what they are thinking and is free to express themself as an Honest Self. Unfortunately in some circumstances, such openness can be a setup for a backlash of negativity; therefore, the Real Self will stay intact yet may only speak up should their ideas, perspectives, or values be at risk of being diminished.

Freedom to openly express as one's Honest Self conveys a general level of low inhibition, while other self-types might proceed with caution. Publicly sharing parts of our Core Self may ignite varying degrees of positive reciprocation from others, thus creating mutual acceptance. In other words, being open and somewhat vulnerable might make it feel safer for others to share more of their own Core Self. Joining with others in this way usually implies we can be open to different personality types along with a willingness to see differing goals and aims of others. We are social beings, and we can benefit from our social interactions. The key is to have acceptance of others and not let go of our own Core Self.

Embracing Self and Others

Positive human connection is experienced when there is a feeling of mutual acceptance. We have an innate drive for affiliation; connecting with others helps us move toward initiating and maintaining interpersonal relationships. The importance of self-acceptance is an essential step in having mutual acceptance. Through this, we experience higher levels of confidence and increased value for ourselves. Self-acceptance also decreases feelings of self-doubt. A healthy belief in one's self is an affirmation of one's Core Self. Feeling free to share the Self while acknowledging and accepting the ways of others is an important factor when engaging in relationships through open communication.

A former female client struggled with her own self-acceptance. She typically distanced herself from honest, natural impulses that varied from the norm. Whenever she did not join along with the group consensus, she felt out of place and carried strong feelings of self-doubt. She weighed the options of appreciating her inner Core Self or working to outwardly fit in with different groups to align with their opinions, beliefs, or ideologies.

The advantage of fitting in meant she would feel some level of acceptance from the outside. However, she also recognized that by doing this, there could be a price to pay. Fitting in often meant she would give up parts of her identity and not feel congruent between thoughts, feelings, beliefs, and actions. Being her Core Self meant she would be real and not struggle to belong to those groups with which she was interacting. She also might not feel group acceptance, which felt really uncomfortable. Choosing a Real or Honest Self stance might result in consequences she wanted to avoid, such as rejection.

Can we make decisions about choosing between Core Self fidelity or adapting to uncomfortable social norms? The choice to be one's Core Self can be difficult, especially for those who clearly have unique personalities instead of those who are more passive and agreeable. The stronger the personality, the more difficult it might be to comply with a group mentality where there is less in common.

Those struggling to determine their social stance when associating with different groups of people may easily relate to the woman discussed. Choosing to embrace one's Core Self is a start in being real. However, there are others who clearly seek acceptance from the outside and will usually prefer joining with the dominant group identity.

The Challenge of Revealing the Self

On the surface, joining the dominant group seems easier and minimizes conflict with others. It additionally creates an artificial feeling of inclusion within the group. There are also those who may choose group affiliation but feel uncomfortable with the added feelings of anxiety produced from incongruity. These individuals will experience emotional dissonance that ironically may steadily draw them in to learn the value of their own uniqueness and individuality.

When trying to portray oneself as someone other than their Core Self, there might be anxiousness and difficulty relaxing, considering that they are not behaving in the way they would behave naturally. Constant management of thoughts and feelings are often necessary because these individuals are mostly behaving as a Lost or Hidden Self. One may feel guarded and even vigilant while maintaining communications that are unnatural. When people continuously portray ungenuine thoughts or feelings, all that is inside and not expressed can become overwhelming. They might repress their unwanted feelings or even act them out.

Sometimes the resultant emotional effect may be a person with extreme expressiveness. For some repressed individuals, the repercussions can be "blowing up." For others, the outcome may be expressed through emotional hurt to the point of acute sadness. Whatever the emotion, the end experience varies for each individual and ultimately correlates to the individual's temperament. Even if we deny our feelings temporarily, they will eventually be expressed to relieve us of what has been withheld.

At times it feels safer to conceal inner thoughts and feelings. It seems safer when meant as emotional self-protection as well as a means of shielding others from potentially extreme reactive emotion. Though most of us can manage moderate levels of acting falsely, there may be a tipping point where buried emotions are expressed. Keeping silent about inner thoughts that oppose the group and are self-deceiving can eventually deplete a person of their usual coping mechanisms and lower their frustration tolerance. This is best understood when trying to manage uncomfortable and incongruent feelings as a Hidden Self.

By withholding our true nature, we are actively suppressing certain thoughts and feelings. Such guarded behavior can become wearing when it is a repetitive suppression over time. This might explain why someone "breaks down" and cries, "loses their temper," or "unexpectedly blows up." Reactions may seem out of proportion to simple situations. The buildup of suppressed emotion may overtake what is unseen and cannot be contained by the person.

When we subconsciously repress as a Lost Self or actively suppress as a Hidden Self, there is a potential for displaced emotions that might be expressed verbally through negativity, criticism, or sarcasm. It may also be displayed nonverbally through facial expression and other physical behaviors. By burying our Core Self's expression, we limit the process of sharing who we are as individuals: a healthy person who should be valued.

Lost Self = Repression (Subconscious)

Hidden Self = Suppression (Intentional Avoidance)

The Real Self may sometimes conceal personal views or opinions that do not match with a group mentality. This is different from the Hidden Self, since the Real Self has a purpose with the goal of not agitating others or creating conflict when it is not necessary. As a Real Self, a person is not hiding or giving up their personal values. The individual is still aware of personal thoughts and feelings with clarity. They really know what they think and feel, which is a real and honest experience. However, a Real Self might choose to filter what they internally experience and not stir up issues through revealing themself. This is to avoid discord or friction coming from the inflexible reactions of others or to avoid being misunderstood.

Presenting as a Real Self with personal limits may be of benefit to both oneself and the people with whom one engages. Here it is not necessary to hide the Core Self while the individual still remains aware of who they are and does not compromise their values. Maintaining boundaries with openness can be rewarding when trying to join or connect with others. The Real Self individual may choose to consciously filter certain thoughts and feelings, and decide what is important to share. Groups may or may not show a genuine interest in the unique views or ideas of an individual, but if questioned, a Real Self will openly share. Groups are either within family systems or social communities, such as friends, work associates, and other organizations.

Behaving as an Honest Self encompasses many of the highlights of the Real Self but with less of a conscious filter. Such a person is less concerned over how others perceive them. They feel free to openly express thoughts and feelings with a reduced fear of reactions from the group. General norms may still be respected by the Honest Self, but these individuals are comfortable disagreeing or behaving as they choose. Their decisions are usually clear and opinions are conveyed overtly. They are operating from a place of sincerity, and they are earnest in what they share.

Honest Self individuals feel free to communicate from a natural place of expression, with some using gut instinct rather than reasoning or logic to make decisions. They appear to believe in their decisions with strong conviction and feel that their decisions are a better representation of their true Self. Studies have shown that participants who made gut decisions felt more confident of their choices and are more likely to advocate for them. Decisions based on feelings appear to represent what people perceive within themselves and may be closely aligned with the concept of the Core Self.

Risks of Rejection

There are some individuals who respond to a person's Honest Self by criticizing, shunning, or rejecting them. Negative consequences are common for those who have free expression that is not comfortably aligned with the general ideas or norms of the dominant group. Direct or subtle shaping often occurs as a simple means of drawing a person into the group mentality. Though it opens the door for group inclusion, it also means that the person is now more likely to behave as a Hidden Self. If the person resists joining the group mentality, they are likely revealing thoughts, feelings, or values that do not coincide with the group.

Sometimes others fear thoughts, skills, or talents of free and unreserved individuals, which might be experienced as intimidating. This may exist when one's unique abilities place them in a position of prominence or when it is believed that their extraordinary skills might surpass others. Such an expertise or high ability merely separates individuals by talent, but the skill does not define the individual. Our Core Self is a combination of many variables within several parts of the Self. We are so much more than the temperaments and traits that contribute to who we are.

Honest Self individuals usually show comfort when sharing who they are, and they will reveal their strengths as well as weaknesses. It is more difficult to do this when a person with distinct abilities does not feel they fit well within the group. This is also true for individuals with unique problems or impairments. Their differences from the group could be embraced and supported, but they may also feel rejected. For those individuals who have some type of physical, emotional, or thought-processing problem, it may be challenging to completely be themselves, especially if they feel judged and at risk for nonacceptance. Behaving as an Honest Self requires courage, particularly when the outcome may be group exclusion rather than inclusion.

Individuals within society may condemn or ridicule others with a special uniqueness. Being unique becomes bad. Mediocre seems acceptable. People may feel they are pulled away from their individuality and should not show their true Self. Being one's Core Self will not be welcomed by everyone. We see this starting with young school children. They are sometimes mocked when they present as different.

Some children may feel pressured to follow others for peer approval and acceptance. As a result, they may try to join with popular friends to fit in and avoid group exclusion. Children often learn to handle this type of conformity from their peers. The pain of ridicule or rejection can convince a youngster to acquiesce and accept norms because norms seem expected. Such actions are reinforced by social culture, and they are carried on from the childhood schoolyard through adolescence and into adulthood.

Following social norms usually benefits the individual and society. Norms represent the values, beliefs, and actions that are accepted as normal within a group. In some ways, they delineate the guiding principles of what is acceptable within a society and how people should behave. Getting along within a community of people creates bonding. It also helps establish rules that are either clearly stated or unspoken. However it becomes more complicated when a subgroup of society operates with different rules and an individual feels conflicted about joining the group.

It is more complex when the individual must act incongruently with his or her Self to conform. Accepting new norms may be tricky, generally because one may withhold personal opinions or change their values to try to belong. This can inhibit emotional development, since it prevents a person from attaining their own growth potential. Conversely, when we feel comfortable as ourselves, we might flourish with skills and talents that are unseen when operating as a Lost or Hidden Self.

Traits: Common and Unique

It is important to appreciate that each of us possesses unique strengths and has had personal successes at various times in our life. Such accomplishments may be presented at varying levels of skill proficiency therefore may not always be acknowledged as something good. Further, recognizing our own unique abilities as positive characteristics may be hard for the Self to accept. Sometimes when skills come naturally, a person is uncomfortable believing that their own strengths are special. This is when self-acceptance is important. It allows an individual to appreciate their own uniqueness. Reciprocal acceptance between Self and others should also be valued, since it is nonjudgmental and mutually encouraging. It occurs when we demonstrate open-mindedness and tolerance toward others and receive the same in return.

Even though we have not all had similar opportunities to succeed to the best of our abilities, an open, social approach to others with positive intent is meaningful. Under these conditions, a person can feel good about who they are as well as help support others to be their Core Self. We are not meant to be replicas of each other. Though we may experience some common traits with others, there are aspects of ourselves that are truly unique, whether it's a single characteristic or a combination that contributes to our individuality.

Most traits are common, yet some traits may appear as unique within certain people. In a graphic depiction of this, we should see most of us appearing close to the middle in what is called a normal distribution or bell curve.

The majority of individuals will fit into 68 percent of the bell curve for most trait behaviors and personal characteristics. Our commonness will be within the range of one standard deviation to the left or right of the bell curve center (mean). Perhaps from a group perspective, being close to the center might be described as ideal. This relates to any descriptor that is measurable for an individual. "Perfect," in this form, can be defined as average and also nonthreatening.

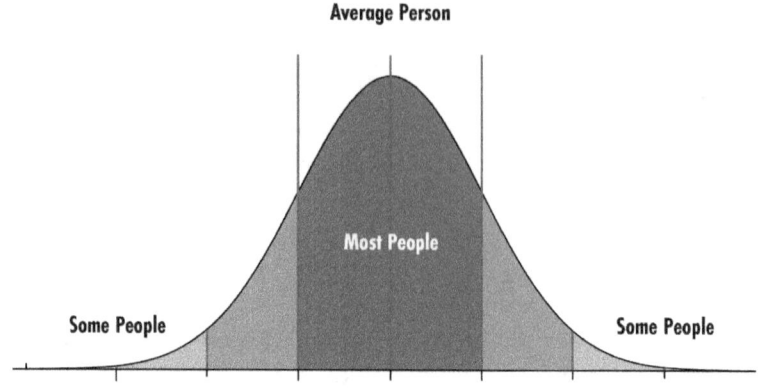

Figure 4. Appearance of common and unique traits within a normal distribution.

As an individual demonstrates other, more unique characteristics and abilities, they move further away from the general ways of others, which might appear a little or extremely different. These unique trait differences are rare, with only a small percent of the population landing plus or minus two or three standard deviations from the mean (outliers). Imagine how unique a person may be with a particular ability that is present or accessible in only a small percentage of the population. Special skills, as well as certain disabilities, will land in this portion of the bell curve.

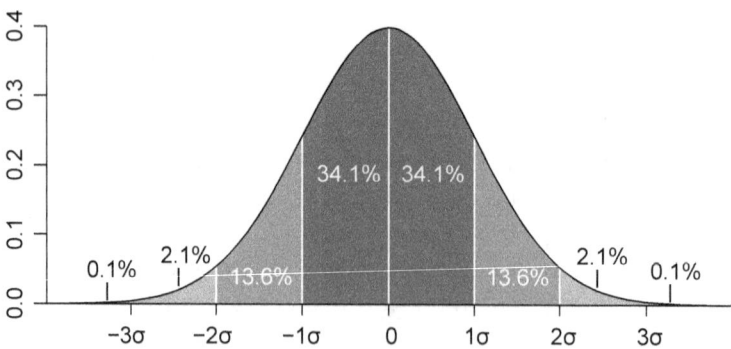

Figure 5. Standard deviations in traits, behaviors, and personality characteristics.

There are times when uniqueness related to individuality is unwelcomed. This usually occurs when a personal trait, style, opinion, or value does not align with the mainstream. It is here that a person may become an outlier to the group. Conventional or popular beliefs and trends are sometimes valued more than originality. Only a select few seem entitled to freely express views that vary from the larger group.

Some individuals may have achieved a certain status that permits them to follow their own style without opposition. Here, a person may behave as a Real or Honest Self with little to no judgment. They may come across as a "straight shooter" who speaks their mind or is considered a little eccentric but with creativity or wisdom. Some of these individuals have earned positions of power and are minimally concerned or affected by the consequences that may exist for their openness. They may also carry a role that receives respect. This can often be seen with elders or those who have many years of experience in a particular occupation or special life experience. They are given more flexibility and freedom to be their Core Self, and the group will usually not challenge them. They essentially get a "pass" and receive Individualistic Freedom without hindrance or restraint. They are allowed a special deviation from group norms without consequences.

Sometimes these individuals appear loose and unfettered with their openness. With such Individualistic Freedom comes responsibility. Making remarks with socially inappropriate content can occur, but when a person is held in high status the group may let it go and will sometimes even embrace what is said. However, should the average person attempt to share a similar and unsuitable thought, they may have problems with the group.

Another example of this phenomenon is seen when someone who has Individualistic Freedom makes a suggestion to the group that might be deemed as simplistic, uncreative, illogical, or even offensive. The suggestion is commonly taken seriously and can become part of the group discussion. Should the average person propose something similar, they might be ignored or minimal value is placed on the suggestion. Sometimes this average person will make a reasonably beneficial recommendation. But if they are not valued, the idea might be ignored. When the same idea is then presented by one who has Individualistic Freedom, the group may opt to give attention to the "new" idea.

The concept of Idiosyncrasy Credits is another way people are enabled with the freedom to act as a Real or Honest Self. Oftentimes when an individual has joined a group and maintains compliance with group norms, they are later deserving of the privilege to deviate from the norms. In essence, they have built up credits that they may use when needed.

Through loyalty to a group, a person may develop a social status permitting variance from general group expectations. Though the person has a history of conformity with the group, Idiosyncrasy Credits may elevate the person's standing and give them the freedom to express themself honestly. This may be seen in large extended families, work settings, or social situations. What is interesting is that this individual has a choice to express as they choose or may withhold and maintain a Hidden Self mentality.

Individuals viewed as eccentric typically struggle to gain acceptance and join in ordinary relationships within a group. These individuals tend to behave in ways that others might consider different. Their Honest Self comes with a unique style and personal opinions that are unlike those of most people, since they think and act in unconventional ways. This person typically thinks creatively but sometimes breaks the status quo. They struggle to be accepted because they are misunderstood by individuals who become too uncomfortable entertaining what might actually be refreshing group contributions.

With eccentricity comes openness and a creative drive. Such a person's uniqueness may convey that they are less likely to imitate others. They will not follow group norms easily, such as out of obligation or social need. They usually operate honestly with little distancing from their Core Self.

When examining the conventional ways to achieve goals within a group, there are usually some unwritten rules with a formula to utilize and follow. The steps to achieve acceptable goals are reinforced by the group's members. However, creative thinkers will usually choose the path less taken. They function more independently, since they are unique and unlikely to follow a standard structure that becomes routinely replicated.

Choosing a personal and unique approach will sometimes increase the odds of success, since the person is following their own path with the skills that are innate and true to their Core Self. Unfortunately, this is not always welcomed, and the individual may experience negative feedback or consequences. Sometimes the usual way of doing things is noncontroversial and more welcomed by the group. It may also be repetitious with low creativity and low reward.

Certain Core Self attributes may be diminished or absent when one chooses to follow generally accepted rules within a group system. The uniqueness of the individual may get discouraged through direct and indirect ways, which means individuality is not embraced. In this situation, movement toward openness is unlikely. The implied rules set by the outside reduce originality from emerging within individuals. This may occur within small groups, various organizations, and larger communities.

Even though all societies operate within laws and social order, a free society should encourage the special uniqueness for each of its members. However, limitations to openness and freedom to be as oneself can be seen within so many social classifications, including small peer groups of children to large organizations run by adults. Further, all countries who have well-developed educational systems for learning also utilize their schools to help develop the country's common national identity. This also helps to keep order and maintain social norms. Other systems, such as the workplace, create rules for others to follow so there is structure along with clear expectations.

It is best when various groups are open to new ideas, especially when group leaders, or those with some form of power, are supportive and accepting of individual creativity. However, there are those who are discouraging and create a dilemma for the individual: "If I follow group expectations, will I still have opportunities to share new ideas?" or "Am I able to approach certain tasks in different ways without disrespecting group norms?" The answers are not simple, since they bring up other questions related to the appropriateness of new ideas and generating a paradigm alteration. It also creates a new evaluation of what are acceptable boundaries and whether group thinking and expectations can be redefined.

Creative Individuality or Stuck with Inaction

Generally, it is important to comply with established rules within group organizations, but there may also be proper occasions when Core Self congruency can fit a situation. In other words, there are times when we can feel comfortable showing parts of our Real Self to the group. Periodically, we make choices that seem simple and uncomplicated. Sometimes the result ends with negative consequences, yet other times there is success.

For instance, when a person tries to establish themselves within a new group of individuals who have common interests, they usually enter from the outside, since they are not currently an existing part of the group. They become aware of the group's general approach to life circumstances yet may also have their own skill set and personal drive. Choosing to approach problems and situations differently than the group may feel risky. A personal approach may leave a person feeling alone. Though the safest route is to keep within established limits, the reward from a more creative approach may result in a greater payoff. Here, the creative person is also being true to themself and allowing their inner Core Self to be revealed.

One illustration of Core Self freedom can be seen through the following scenario: An immigrant who is settling into their new country has limitations with language, education, social engagement, and support systems. Initially, their reference group will be with others of a similar cultural background and work experience. They see that there are various opportunities for monetary success in their trade or profession, but they must find a means of making their own circumstances for success possible. Acting as a Core Self, they maintain their values and allow their creativity to grow. If they choose a safer route to earning a living, the process might be slower and less reward-ing. Following the same path of those with similar conditions may draw in group support but may not be beneficial or fulfilling. Through hard work, savings, making the right connections, and even showing certain respected values, they might succeed, where homegrown, educated citizens might fail in their same field. They do not follow a scripted process. They know what they know. They use the skills that are theirs. They tap into parts of their Core Self for success to thrive.

Some of my clients view their future idealistically in terms of success. Though this is motivating and positive, their approach in achieving their objectives is often limited. They sometimes work toward their goals as a Lost Self, restricting themselves through formulas laid out by their accomplished pre-decessors. If they are to use critical thinking and creative skills, they might find their own success in their particular field. But over time, several of these clients develop negative self-feelings preventing them from success. Their lack of productivity is their limitation. If they accept that they have their own unique talents with skills to achieve their goals, they might succeed. Instead, they may feel stuck in a state of inertia, since there are obstacles that seem insurmountable.

The idea of creating and managing steps toward a desired goal can be exciting. This occurs when creativity is released and a person feels empow-ered by initiating their own individualized approach. Feeling stuck can be remedied by opening up the mind and allowing the Self to explore avenues that may appear closed but are merely unexplored. Though it is true that not all creative ventures will end in a Nobel Prize, it is also true that there are definite wins and opportunities present when one chooses to approach things differently among colleagues and peers. They must be focused and stay on track with their goal.

Oftentimes we will experience hurdles or disruptions along the way. Other times there are huge roadblocks preventing a smooth transition from one part of the journey to the next. However, there are many ways to get past a brick wall. To get to the other side, one must choose what is best for them. If I cannot break through the wall, I might try to go over it, under it, around the left or right, or even dismantle it piece by piece. Sometimes I need help from others to get to the other side. Whatever the case, we should do our best to get to where we need to go as ourselves.

Another example of distancing from the Core Self relates to a young adult male client who was frustrated with his acting career. Jarod experienced mild anxiety and was struggling with his approach to getting work in the movie industry. He, like many other actors, believed that to be successful, he must take certain scripted steps to achieve his goal. The formula for many actors seems to combine specific options of action. Jarod's options seemed more like expectations he needed to fulfill so he could enter the industry properly.

Common backgrounds for actors include taking college acting courses, enrolling with improvisational acting troupes, learning method or classical acting from some famous/experienced actor, attending a reputable program producing successful actors, working as a movie extra, as well as working as a waiter in a prestigious, high-end Hollywood restaurant. Though these measures seem stereotypical for actors, many will often engage in these steps to achieve their goal.

Actors' portfolios include much of the same with typical replications by so many others. After all this, they also contribute to peripheral industries by getting professional photos and working with managers and agents to get readings for an acting role. Some view these activities as part of "paying your dues," yet it is essentially following the same formula of fellow actors on the same route with the same goal.

The industry is flooded with talented actors. Following others with a common approach in procuring acting roles is faulty, since it takes away from real creativity. The actor then becomes dependent mostly on luck to succeed.

Jarod was doing what the rest of his peers were doing. He did not consider how following a scripted formula actually made it more difficult for others to notice his unique talent.

Ironically, the industry seems to want uniqueness, yet Jarod was one of many "typicals" and did not share much of who he really was as an individual. Eventually, Jarod was able to tap into his own creativity and explore different ways to approach his acting career. He behaved more as a Real Self. This helped him behave congruently and feel less anxious. He worked on alternative ideas to be known as an actor and increased his opportunities for success.

An individual who chooses to think outside the box may feel like an outlier and could experience group exclusion, however they may also encounter fewer obstacles in their journey. Here they are making their way through a style of life that better matches their personal skills and eliminates another standard plan that is less familiar to them. Conventional ways may actually be more difficult and discouraging. This can lead one into falsely believing that they are failures and questioning why they struggle to advance in a career or activity when they should experience success. It is far more beneficial and healthier to engage in interactions where one is being their Core Self instead of accepting uncomfortable rules set by social norms. Though the road may appear long and arduous, there is value in approaching goals in a personal manner that are congruent with the Self.

Struggles with Incongruity

There are benefits to self-congruence, especially for those with high levels of self-acceptance. Such individuals have determined that what they think and feel are theirs, and they can choose how to share who they are with others. These individuals tend to have high levels of compassion and can empathize with others while offering acceptance without moral judgments. Unfortunately, it can seem isolating when one offers support and acceptance to others yet is interacting with people who do not share similar values. Further, one can also feel disconnected to an individual or group, based on their disingenuous presentations. Oftentimes insincere individuals operate almost mechanically, unaware of the negative impact they project.

Understanding the concept of incongruity is important, since it is a result of people who are not consistently meshed with their thoughts, feelings, or actions and are disconnected from their Core Self. It also creates negative feelings related to a double bind. When portraying the Self publicly as one way but actually thinking and feeling a different way, there is uncertainty about what is a true reality. This relates to Hidden Self individuals.

Those who recognize the incongruity of a dual communication may be confused and even frustrated. Sometimes expressed double bind messages are realized consciously, however they can also be perceived subconsciously. Insincerity is an example of this. A person presenting as positive and helpful, yet who is also behaving as withholding and unsupportive, is creating a double bind message. Their behavior may be incongruent with their verbal statements and nonverbal actions. The receiver of the conflicting messages is not clear if they are in the presence of a Hidden or Real Self and misunderstands the individual's behavior or intent.

When people behave in a fake and insincere manner, they are projecting a false Self to others. For example, there was a young female client who shared her discomfort over a recent call made to her by a close family friend. The friend called this client to express her concern about an earthquake that just hit an area in Southern California where the client resided. The woman said all the right things, such as "Is everything OK?" and "We were worried about you." However, her reaching out and her concern took place a day after being informed of the quake. The woman also segued into unrelated questioning about other issues that were personal. The questions were unrelated to the purpose of the initial contact.

The client stated in therapy that she felt uneasy and confused about the family friend's concerns. This was based on the incongruity of the person's presentation. Though it was possible that the flow of conversation could have naturally shifted from the initial subject to other information, the actual perception verbalized by the client was how insincere the contact felt. Here, we have an interesting dynamic of perceived conflictual messages interpreted as insincerity.

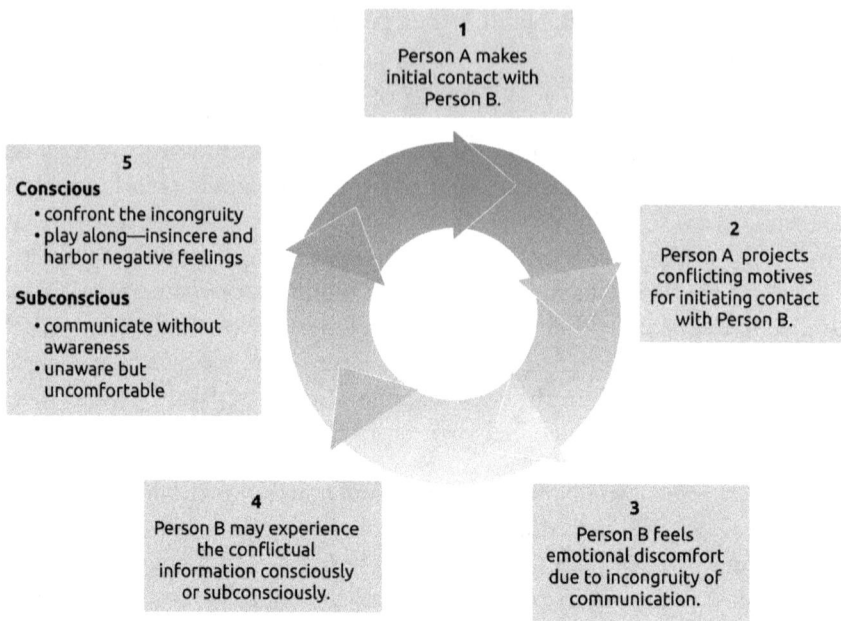

1
Person A makes initial contact with Person B.

2
Person A projects conflicting motives for initiating contact with Person B.

3
Person B feels emotional discomfort due to incongruity of communication.

4
Person B may experience the conflictual information consciously or subconsciously.

5
Conscious
• confront the incongruity
• play along—insincere and harbor negative feelings

Subconscious
• communicate without awareness
• unaware but uncomfortable

Figure 6. Cycle of incongruent communication.

The above cycle demonstrates how mixed communications may be experienced by a receiving party. When communications are consistently incongruent, such as with double bind messages, the receiver of the communications may question themself about whether they understand things accurately. When they feel safe enough to address incongruent communication, there is an opportunity to gain more clarity or whittle the information down to the honest basics of the exchange. However, when they feel stuck and cannot comment on the incongruity, they may experience emotional stress.

Whether we are aware or unaware of mixed messages in communication, we are usually trying to make sense of them and process what was presented. Sometimes we experience an internal reaction to incongruent communication. Being aware of this may be an important insight, as it helps to explain certain negative emotional reactions we might have.

Incongruent communication is hard to engage, and it can pull one into behavior that is more of a Hidden Self type just to get along. This is because the incongruent person is withholding genuine communications. They often deny who they really are or what they feel, thus further distancing the receiver from an honest reality.

Understanding Dysfunctional Communication

There are some individuals who create chaos with mixed messages, especially when their communication is complex and involves more than one person. Here, the receivers have a difficult time managing reality, since communication is loaded with misinformation. The instigators of such messy situations are either Lost or Hidden Selves. Their behavior may at times be conscious. Other times they operate subconsciously yet still disturb open and honest communication.

As a receiver of mixed messages, it may seem confusing and it can also plant ideas of doubt. The process is very similar to the Cycle of Incongruent Communication discussed above. It can become more complex when multiple people feed into the dysfunction. Therapeutically, it is important to examine the intent of the metamessages and what is being insinuated by words.

Manipulative communication with mixed messages seems easier to identify and decipher when it is obvious and intentional. The communicator might even feel a sense of pride when maneuvering successfully in situations where the person achieves more than one goal, such as "killing two birds with one stone." Unfortunately, a receiver of such dysfunctional communication may encounter self-doubt and also experience unfamiliar emotions due to the incongruity felt. If one is only listening to what is said, they can accept or reject the basic words as stated. However, humans are more complex; we pick up other communications, whether or not they are understood and accepted.

An example of this type of communication relates to a client's sixty-seven-year-old parent named Samuel. He applied manipulative communication within his family, using great skill. He managed to have positive and negative effects on several people simultaneously. For instance, Samuel told his forty-two-year-old daughter Amy the following directive: "Please tell your sister, Lisa, I'm not up for talking these days." Such a simple sentence is loaded with data. Here is the back story: Lisa had been calling her father, Samuel, to see how he is doing. This loving daughter is expected to make regular phone contacts, since she lives far away. When she doesn't call, Samuel uses guilt tactics to manipulate the daughter, so Lisa calls several times a week. Amy, the other daughter, behaves like a child with her father. She is not married but is currently in a significant relationship with her boyfriend. Samuel uses this daughter to communicate to family members as a control tactic.

The following metacommunications are made through Samuel's single statement through Amy:

- *Amy is privileged to be her father's spokesperson. She is placed in a special role within the family.*

- *Amy is also special since her father is able or still wants to talk to her.*

- *Because Amy is so special, she is willing to work hard to please Samuel.*

- *Something does not seem right with Samuel . . . Is he ill? Is he depressed? Lisa worries about her father's condition.*

- *Speaking to Lisa may make things worse for Samuel, so their communication is suspended.*

- *There is no end stated about Samuel's current request of noncommunication with Lisa, and with such vagueness, it creates anxiety.*

- *Discussions are started among Lisa and other siblings who have had similar recent communications from Samuel through Amy. This creates additional worry and confusion over what to do.*

- *Other family members attempt to speak to Samuel but get minimal feedback. Samuel receives increased attention.*

Samuel's behavior was clearly manipulative. He used his power position as a parent to communicate vague directives to his children for some goal or purpose. With such vagueness, Lisa was confused over what to do, unclear if boundaries should be followed, and unaware if she actually did something wrong or hurtful to her father. The lack of information conjured up ideas that something was not right, and it drew in the other siblings. With such dysfunctional patterns of communication, a child may feel they are "going crazy."

Handling this has limited options. Ideally, the inconsistencies could be confronted. This is only beneficial when the instigator is willing to discuss issues properly. The other approach can be an honest sharing of feelings, meaning one can express how mixed messages feel, as well as vague, indirect communication.

It is critical that the receiver of manipulations and mixed messages be aware of their own thoughts and feelings instead of assuming a role within the dysfunctional system. If the other person is unwilling to accept responsibility or does not recognize that their communication is a problem, the receiver should not continue to engage the dysfunctional system and instead should try to move forward. By doing so, they can operate as their Real Self and not compromise their values or feed into another person's negative behavior.

The Core Self should not be diminished in a way that pulls the person out of their true character to simply get along with others. They will not benefit by behaving incongruently. Merely recognizing and accepting how one feels can motivate them to remain true to who they are. A direct and honest approach may also help to set important limits and establish healthy boundaries, but it must be done consistently over time.

It is sometimes uncomfortable when trying to be supportive and open-minded with individuals who do not exchange a similar level of care and awareness. It is most beneficial to still engage others as your Core Self, but it may also bring out feelings of resentment and frustration due to a low level of reciprocity. If communication feels one-sided and repeatedly serves the needs of one person, a change may be needed.

This is not to say that an individual should change their values. Instead, they might benefit by appropriately addressing what is bothering them, while maintaining their Core Self. This approach is best with open, factual statements. Through this type of connection a person is less likely to engage in negative emotions such as anger. It is important to express ourselves clearly without changing who we are. The Core Self should remain stable and not change.

I had a client, James, who had a positive connection with a friend who became an active member of James's family. James and his friend were like brothers, each one supporting the other on simple things like projects, borrowing tools, and taking each other and their families to the airport when necessary, the kind of friend you can depend on, as you would depend on a family member. They shared a solid friendship and seemed mutually supportive when the need to talk about personal issues arose.

Unfortunately, what appeared as an equal friendship over the years was actually a little lopsided. Their friendship was unbalanced considering that James's buddy constantly had struggles and frequently dominated their conversations with his personal life situations. James admittedly had co-dependency traits, such as poor boundaries and caretaking. He recognized that he felt compelled to help others who were suffering and frequently worked harder than they would to resolve their own issues, usually sacrificing even his own needs to help. This was clearly the case with James's support toward his close friend.

Through processing his concerns in therapy, James verbalized feelings of frustration and resentment. This was because he genuinely cared and gave so much of his time and emotional energy. In the end, there was very little support reciprocated to James when he himself was struggling or was in a rough spot. James did not want to completely change his Core Self, including the behavior that kept him present for his friend. He did not want to distance himself from who he truly was as an individual. He still felt it was important to offer support through active consideration and care. This included active listening skills accompanied by problem-solving with thoughtful recommendations.

However, since James began feeling resentful toward his friend, he was unhappy. Though his approach initially came from a place of genuine caring, he felt their friendship was not appropriately balanced. He stated that he felt "burned out," and he decided to address his feelings directly to his friend. James's intent was to speak to his friend about his personal feelings of frustration. He wanted to emphasize that at times when he brought up his own personal matters, his friend minimized or dismissed them.

James eventually initiated a conversation with his friend about how he was feeling. Following the discussion there was a distance between the two men. Though they still had some level of contact, their friendship was not the same. This was due to the limits and boundaries James created. James had mixed feelings about their new connection. He still cared for his friend but also needed to care for himself. James felt he had grown through his insights; he asserted himself and remained congruent with his Core Self. He never rejected his friend, but he was able to honestly share what his needs were. This was done with factual statements and not through accusations or expressions on an emotional level.

Several months after the change in his friendship, a close relative of James's friend unexpectedly passed away. In therapy, James shared how reaching out to his friend came naturally. He did not want to feel incongruent and stated, "I'd like him to know I care, but I have to stop overextending myself."

James chose to write a note of condolences with a sincere acknowledgment of what his friend and family must be going through emotionally. In the past, he might have spent a lot of time with his friend, as well as talk to him regularly on the phone as a support.

James felt strange since he believed he was operating slightly out of character. Though he remained his Real Self, there were elements of his behavior that had changed. Previously, he would have chosen to step in and be the caretaker, which all would have expected. Instead he felt incongruent, which prompted him to reach out as his Real Self. He realized that withholding support was not how he would naturally respond, yet he could now maintain better boundaries for himself.

In therapy he stated that he felt his behavioral change created a distancing from his Core Self, yet he also believed the change was necessary. It was good to have this insight, since it reinforced that he was not acting impulsively. Instead, he was changing internal negative feelings experienced from communicating with others in ways that increased frustration and resentment.

James had a history of overextending himself to others who often took advantage of his good nature and kindness. Unfortunately, with his close friend, the asymmetrical exchanges were wearing on him. Through this, James recognized his history of developing friendships with people who have high needs and gave him minimal support in return.

Behaving in new ways that are based on uncomfortable thoughts and feelings can cause a person to feel incongruent. This is true for those who decide to change their communication and action based on various levels of negative responses received. When we shut down parts of our true nature, we may not feel normal. Instead we might feel fake since we are not acting in ways that come from our natural instinct.

Unfortunately, some of us are such good actors that we may lose that real inner awareness of what our identity truly is. Our new presentation could result in a shift in how we approach others. Therefore, Core Self awareness is always important and can be better realized through a Real Self presentation. We can learn to get back to the Core Self through psychosocial insights and personal introspection.

Developing Healthier Relationships

Realize that when we are fake, we are not our natural selves and we suffer the consequences. Through this incongruity of the Self, some of us develop varying degrees of discomfort related to anxiety and depression. Anxiety fits well as a repercussion of being a Lost Self. Conflicting thoughts and feelings become a battle, leaving one to be stuck through incongruence. Negative reflection of the Self may also cause feelings of depression.

Fortunately, certain depressive symptoms may fade or vanish over time, especially when we resort back to a Real Self mentality. However, even when behaving as a Real Self, other familiar consequences may emerge, causing a person to feel sad and discouraged for being themselves, such as with social disapproval. This is what was avoided in the first place, but now the individual is more congruent. They will benefit by working on their relationships with others who may be accepting, rejecting, or afraid of the emerging Core Self of that individual.

Within a healthy relationship, a positive development is likely in reference to the acceptance of one's Self and the acceptance of others. Socially, group and individual connections to people should improve through one's emotional growth and mutual acceptance toward one another. Each relationship has its own challenges, but a common theme relates to trust and feeling comfortable enough to openly reveal the Self with the hope of unconditional acceptance; this is especially true within intimate relationships. If there is a history of hurtful or negative social interactions, it may be difficult to trust the motives of others. It is especially true for someone who has experienced distressing emotional wounds from the past. It is reasonable to assume that one would be guarded as a means of preventative self-protection.

A thirty-year-old female client named Evelyn described feelings of anxiety and sadness related to her current relationship because "it was going so well." In fact, it was probably the healthiest of all her past relationships. She stated, "The closer I get to him, the more I worry; the more I worry, the more damage I do in the relationship." Damage, in this case, meant shutting down and pulling away with no explanation for the boyfriend. This type of behavior was a defense that Evelyn developed from past unhealthy relationships that were either abusive or involved an aloof partner.

In this particular relationship, Evelyn recognized that her healthy relationship allowed her to feel a greater sense of trust; however, with this increase of trust, less armor was needed to protect her feelings. This in turn meant that her increased trust also included personal vulnerability. Her trust in her boyfriend could leave her open to being hurt if they were to have an argument or if he were to express himself to her with negative emotions. Trust felt good. But the anticipation of being hurt, as she typically was in the past, could feel worse, since their relationship had become even closer.

The solution to this dilemma was to remind the client that "in this relationship, you can be yourself." Evelyn did not really need to "try," as she did in past relationships. Trying might be a sign that she still feels the need to do something different to please the other person (acting as a Non–Core Self.) Instead, she could be faithful to herself and not try to match another person's needs or directives.

In this relationship, there was positive communication, and the boyfriend was genuine with his feelings. He was very much his Core Self, which made it possible for Evelyn to trust more than she had in previous relationships. The other component to the solution was acknowledgment that she could also reveal her Core Self. This meant self-acceptance and honesty with her thoughts and feelings. Their communication could benefit, and trust would naturally become stronger.

Acceptance of the Core Self is particularly challenging from childhood through early adulthood. Social norms and peer pressures usually trigger insecurities during those years. For some, it may be a struggle throughout their lifetime, especially when denying one's own right to naturally be who they are. Recognizing we each have unique qualities inherent to the Self is a first step in self-acceptance. Appreciating those qualities can be more challenging, but this will be another step toward feeling valued as a person.

Truly being oneself can seem simple, yet it may also add unwanted stress into a person's life. This might happen when we are engaging others who are unaccepting and critical. When encountering such people, group compliance often seems like a safe option, as it is a means of cooperating with social norms and fitting in with group expectations. It also minimizes negative consequences that can emerge when one presents themself as unique or different from the group. Though this option feels safe, it can also create emotional pain, having a negative impact on one's self-esteem. With a false presentation, we are behaving as Hidden Selves without the comfort that comes with self-acceptance.

There are many variables that can instigate feelings of unworthiness along with pressures to behave incongruently with the Self. It is our responsibility to recognize our self-worth and become comfortable revealing who we are among others. We are all individuals who can engage each other with mutual respect and acceptance. While some people respect and accept, others appear as critical and nonembracing of individual uniqueness.

We are all individuals with different ideas and values that are important to us. Though we may have some commonality with others, we do not all think, feel, and act the same. It is good to have self-acceptance. Eventually through personal growth, we will experience mutual acceptance between ourselves and others. This is a part of the process of being our best Selves.

Chapter 8

Finding Your Core Self

Understanding your Core Self is challenging. It may be explored through self-examination and life history insights. It is a process of being completely honest with yourself without creating negative self-judgments. Such self-examination may provide an opportunity to reveal a deeper part of yourself that is oftentimes edited for the sake of outside approval and getting along with others.

When we are young, the Self may be challenged by the incongruence felt between conflicts of the inner Self and life experiences. For example, if a child learns that support and acceptance from their parents is conditional (instead of unconditional), the child learns they will receive support and acceptance only when they behave in certain ways. With this, a child may drift away from what feels natural and act in ways that are more pleasing to others. This may repeat over time and create different approaches to life circumstances. When this occurs there may be feelings of incongruity. The child is stuck somewhere between who they genuinely "are" and how their parents want them to "be." In our early life stages, much of trying to be a certain way is for the sake of receiving parental affection or approval.

When we are being authentic, and there is discouragement from parents or others, we may feel awkward and uncomfortable as ourselves. The message received is that "I am doing something wrong." This may be communicated directly or indirectly. Conversely, supportive parenting is an ideal and should be present from the beginning of a child's life. All forms of communication—whether through spoken words, vocal pitch or tone, physical touch, or facial expressions—convey emotional information that is understood by a child. Encouragement from parents and other significant people in a child's life will also be understood as reassurance. When this is consistent, children feel more confident and congruent.

Sometimes thoughts and feelings that should be expressed naturally become edited to fit outside expectations. Incongruity of the Self will emerge and can hinder an individual's process toward self-acceptance. Sharing oneself honestly is a positive goal. It is closely aligned with one's innate Core Self; however, changes made to revise one's natural Self will ultimately affect the way traits are revealed. Through this understanding, we may want to strive to become reacquainted with our Core Self. Without this understanding, we may experience the discomfort of incongruence.

The Core Self is the purest form of our Real Self. Knowing and accepting our Core Self gives us the freedom to share who we are with honesty. The Core Self is who we currently are and who we were from our past. We are each unique individuals, and no one shares our same set of traits nor their levels of intensity. There are parts of ourselves that have been present and unchanged since early childhood. When we strive to recognize our Core Self and welcome our own genuine thoughts and feelings, we are likely to experience emotional balance. Through self-exploration, we might accept parts of ourselves that have been hidden or dismissed.

Acknowledging the concepts of the Lost and Hidden Self can pave a path toward understanding the Core Self. Though some may struggle with these self-states, they may gain personal insights through honest self-examination. This can help a person understand the limitations to either state of mind. When we are not genuine, we are not our natural selves, and we often endure the consequences of this. With an incongruity of Self, we may experience different amounts of discomfort. Eventually, this may lead to feelings of anxiety and depression.

Embracing one's Core Self can be challenging because of the social pressures for an individual to edit their Core Self. At these times a person can be aware of social influences persuading them to join a group mentality or the pressures made by certain individuals to fit in as something we are not. Remember that the Core Self is who we truly are and that we must learn to appreciate and accept our own unique personal Self qualities.

Acceptance Revisited

There are several variables that create feelings of unworthiness as well as pressures to act incongruently. It is our responsibility to realize our self-value and become comfortable sharing who we are with others. This is self-acceptance. When among others, we should also be able to engage them with acceptance. Some people will understand the value of openness and will respect individuality, while others may not and therefore appear critical and nonembracing of a person's uniqueness.

We are all unique individuals with variations in how we think and feel. Though we may share some similarities with others, we do not all have the same values or ideas. Such differences make us qualitatively different from each other. Understanding this may lead to personal openness and self-acceptance. Ultimately, through this growth we can develop better mutual acceptance between ourselves and others. Through this process we get closer to being our best selves.

In Core Self Theory, self-acceptance is an important factor. It is meant to encourage individuals to recognize and appreciate their true selves. They become aware of how they think and feel within various situations. Experiencing this honestly can bring an individual closer to interacting as their natural inner self with their outside social environment. When this becomes more of a routine standard, the Real Self and Honest Self should emerge. This is a more congruent Self, and an individual is less likely to experience the internal conflicts felt by someone who conceals their personal views, opinions, and actions.

Accepting ourselves as we truly are can lead to certain personal advantages. The value of self-acceptance leads to developing a better, more correct self-image. When we understand ourselves and accept who we are, we will also improve our self-esteem and bolster our confidence. Though at times it may be emotionally difficult to present oneself in ways that do not align with social norms or a dominant group, choosing to be a Real or Honest Self has its own rewards that should not be minimized. Simply put, a Real or Honest Self is not worried about "fitting in" or being discovered as having a false self-presentation. Though at times this person may feel disconnected or ostracized by others for being real or honest, they may also experience clarity of the mind and self-respect from maintaining personal values and opinions that are more congruent with the Self.

As we learn and understand more about our Core Self, we will ideally gain greater self-acceptance and become emotionally healthier within our surroundings. We should feel fewer limitations within social situations because we are presenting more as our Real or Honest Self. As we experience our Core Self through outside social interactions, we may feel an added freedom to be ourselves. Accepting who we are and embracing the same for others is a meaningful objective that eventually helps to enhance mental health and ultimately increases social interest. When we surround ourselves with healthy people who accept the differences of others, there is more opportunity to express oneself naturally and confidently.

Beyond self-acceptance, we must improve our relations with others through mutual acceptance. Sharing support for one another's opinions, viewpoints, and ideas is a form of validation that should prompt feelings of acceptance. Acceptance of others does not always imply agreeability, but it does indicate acknowledgment. Positive relationships exist when there is mutual acceptance.

Connecting with others through acceptance moves us toward initiating and maintaining interpersonal relationships. A healthy belief in one's self is an affirmation of one's Core Self. Feeling free to share the Self while acknowledging and accepting the ways of others is an important factor when engaging in relationships through open communication.

Elements of Our Personality

Individual personalities are a composite of our life histories, genetic makeup, and the more abstract Core Self elements that have existed since we took our first breath of life. These abstract parts of the Self are unique to each individual and relate to our haecceity and temperament. While it is most challenging to properly define a person's haecceity as their true essence, exploring temperament is more measurable and less conceptual. Both of these Core Self elements are the basis of Core Self Theory; together they help define the unique nature of an individual.

Personality Elements:

- **Environmental Factors (life experiences, cultural background, upbringing, trauma)**
- **Traits (genetics)**
- **Temperament (approach to life)**
- **Quiddity (our—humanity's collective—"whatness") and Haecceity (an individual person's "thisness")**

As human beings, we are unique and separate from all other living organisms, which is our quiddity. On a deeper level, our haecceity is our uniqueness that separates us from each other as individuals. On a spiritual level, this may be described as our soul or inner true nature. Our haecceity or soul appears to be an internal part of who we are that goes unchanged. In Core Self Theory, it is recognized that no two individuals are the same. We are each distinctive human beings. Trying to classify individuals into groups or within specific personality categories seems fruitless, as it would disregard the uniqueness of the person.

The other abstract part of the Core Self is our temperament. It includes our emotional disposition as well as our general manner and approach to life. It may be perceived as a style or self-presentation that connects thoughts and feelings within different situations. It also serves to influence trait behavior. Our temperament is important in helping us define who we are and how we operate in our environment.

Temperaments may present in the form of emotional expressiveness. Our temperament may guide us toward the management of our personal dominant traits. Due to our individuality, it is difficult to precisely describe all the distinguishing characteristics encompassed within a person's unique temperament. However, general common features may exist and represent components of our natural Self.

In this model, temperament types are not meant to suggest a personality type descriptor. Instead, they are a resource used as a reference point to help discover our Core Self. If we only consider temperament categories to describe the inner self, we are mistakenly overlooking the complexity of the individual. The element of haecceity is missing. When added together, the essence of who we are as individuals emerges.

Our temperament is evident during the early stages of our lives and influences how we interact with others. Traits are affected by our temperament and have an impact over how we interact with the environment. Our genuine temperament can be shown through personal life experiences in a natural way. For instance, someone who carries an "easy" temperament style might be open and free with expressiveness in a social situation. A "slow to warm" temperament might be cautious and withhold expressiveness in a social situation. The same trait of "expressiveness" is handled differently, depending on the temperament type of the individual.

Whether traits are learned or inherited, they are within us and get presented to the outside world. They are a key component of personality development in addition to the other elements discussed. While some traits are genetically fixed, others may be alterable. A changeable trait could be an attitude or behavior such as thoughtfulness/carelessness or possibly levels of introversion/extroversion. Overall, traits are abundant and represent our basic human presentation. Some traits are significant for an individual and may stand out. Other traits are subtle and may go unnoticed.

Traits are a part of our personality and help us define our sense of Self. Both genetic traits and environmentally developed traits are a part of who we are. Our temperament contributes to the choices we make with our traits. The Core Self expresses the manner in which we think and feel, and ultimately produces actions connected to our traits. We all have a unique combination of traits that are managed through our temperamental approaches. Temperaments are also unique and should be understood in terms of our self-presentation and our interaction with our social environment.

Defining Our Core Self

Haecceity of the Core Self can be considered the foundation of our mind's existence. It drives the Self to be what it is. It is present in every aspect of our lives and influences our temperament, traits, and social life experiences. If one considers their inner Core Self as being developed out of haecceity, temperament, and genetic traits, then they can recognize that a truly unique person exists. Temperaments may be guided by this haecceity or soul with a progression of influence that adjusts our traits. Each of the personality elements should have an impact on an individual's unique self-development.

The ultimate goal of this model is to accept and understand our Core Self. This can be achieved by embracing our inner self as it is. A further goal is to welcome others as they are. Understanding our Core Self is important and best experienced when one can be consistently real. Self-acceptance and acceptance of others should follow.

Some individuals have not experienced real inner awareness and are unclear about what their true identity is. Trying to have Core Self awareness is always important and may be best realized through a Real Self presentation. Psychosocial insights and personal introspection can help us get back to our Core Self. Through this, we may properly engage and value the personal elements of our Core Self. This is because we will feel more congruent. With this deeper self-understanding, we may grow to a level of self-acceptance.

When we struggle to be ourselves in different social situations, we may want to examine our Real Self thoughts and feelings, since they correspond to our deeper Core Self. Asking ourselves "**why** do I think and feel this way?" may not be the best question to ask. Though having personal insight may be important, it does not bring us much closer to defining and understanding our Core Self. The better questions are "**how** am I actually feeling?" and "**what** are my genuine thoughts on this matter?" This will open us up to explore our real thoughts and feelings.

Getting in touch with our Core Self can also be achieved by recalling earlier memories. If you successfully remember how you behaved as a child, you might capture times when your Core Self had more freedom to behave naturally. It might be challenging to mentally enter such remote times of the past, however even glimpses of how you previously approached the world are likely to reveal your Core Self. This would be a time in childhood when you felt free to express yourself with unedited openness as a Real or Honest Self. There was no need for overthinking, second guessing, or negative self-thoughts. You could be real in your thoughts and honest with your expression.

One common reason why we stray from our Core Self is our concern about presenting as "not good enough." We may want to please our parents or meet outside pressures that are not internally authentic. Here, outside expectations do not match with our Real or Honest Self. This may happen if we try to express ourselves in a purely natural way yet discover there is outside disapproval.

Wanting to share an idea or opinion with others may be uncomfortable when there is a fear of disapproval or criticism. In these situations, a person may become guarded and withhold personal thoughts and feelings. They may slip into a Lost or Hidden Self mentality, intending to follow outside expectations rather than accepting their Core Self. Here, the person is wanting to fit in and get along, and gives up their Real or Honest Self presentation to receive false acceptance from the outside.

An example of disapproval or criticism that reshapes the Self is a three-year-old boy wanting to identify with his father by helping him with household chores. If the father is critical or shows annoyance, the boy may feel discouraged and may want to edit his genuine impulse to assist Dad. This may lead to a misdirection of natural thoughts and feelings, thus creating behaviors that are incongruent with his Core Self. The initial focus was to help Dad, which was an authentic desire. However, the boy then may have felt unneeded, which would change his natural motivation. If a pattern continues with similar exchanges, the boy might start to feel and behave incongruently, since he is less of his Real or Honest Self.

We should experience a congruence between our Core Self and how we present ourselves to others. This presentation will be congruent only if our Core Self is welcomed honestly and communication to others is made genuinely. With this level of self-acceptance, harmony should be felt within us. We should then carry a Real Self presence in our life.

Understanding the Need to Return to Our Core Self

Straying from our Core Self increases feelings of incongruity. Letting go of our personal beliefs and true emotions may result in unnatural communications and behaviors. At times we distance ourselves from our Core Self, but this creates a false presentation that can negatively impact us. When we hide the reality of who we are, we are not being real to ourselves and others.

Some individuals may fluctuate between different self-states. Sometimes they are their Real Self but may become a Hidden Self with the intention of fitting in. At times they will have such comfort and familiarity with shifting self-states that it becomes effortless. This person may adapt to their surroundings with the appearance of comfort and acceptance, thus getting along with a group mentality or another's viewpoint that is not their own. A pattern of minimizing the Real or Honest Self can become habitual and subconscious. This is particularly true for those with a Lost Self state. When it becomes persistent with conscious awareness, the person is acting more as the Hidden Self.

When denying our Core Self, we may experience uncomfortable feelings and realize something is emotionally wrong. With incongruity, negative emotions may emerge such as anxiousness, frustration, or depression. Through these feelings, we can explore our Core Self. This may determine if we are in a position contrary to a healthier Real Self presentation. We can examine the four self-states to discern which one best describes our current behavior. Ideally, we should strive to be our Real or Honest Self.

Returning to our Real or Honest Self is challenging, especially if we have become so familiar with the Lost or Hidden Self way of life. Consistent familiarity with a disguised self can seem satisfying. This is because of integrated rewards built-in for behaviors that are aligned with group beliefs and values. Group acceptance is a reward that creates a deeper feeling of group unity.

Belonging to the group can also feel safer. Instead of risking exclusion, we feel welcomed. Such social inclusiveness can sometimes feel easier to manage. It may seem more rewarding to go along with a group mentality instead of sharing thoughts and opinions that differ from a majority. We may feel rejected or disconnected from others when we have different views and we share them openly.

Choosing to reveal our Real Self among others with different ideas can feel risky. Emotional safety becomes an important concept that is significant when considering a possible outcome after sharing genuine thoughts and opinions. Such freedom of expression may have consequences that appear more negative than positive. When personal viewpoints are shared and are unpopular, we may experience unwelcomed repercussions through direct or indirect communications. Ultimately, there may be ramifications for individuality, however there may be greater satisfaction knowing we are being authentic and not acting to fit in.

When to Withhold Our Real/Honest Self

It is important to be aware of feelings for ourselves and others. We can be sensitive to another person's needs and still take care of our own needs. We want to be honest with ourselves in terms of thoughts and feelings, as well as share empathy for the thoughts and feelings of others.

While it seems optimal to have the freedom to express ourselves naturally and without limits, it is also important to have an awareness of the potential effect our communications may have on others. Being our Core Self does not translate to sharing unrestrained expression regardless of the impact it may have on others. Instead we want to have the freedom to be ourselves while also being aware of our impact on others.

Being our Core Self can include mutual respect and understanding of others, even when we have personal differences. When we are socially engaged with others who have different ideas, we must be cognizant of the impact we might have if choosing to be our Honest Self. Communicating with others should be done nonoffensively; it also means choosing what to say and when it is appropriate to speak out. We do not want our honest expression to negatively affect another person.

A Real Self presentation is appropriate for us most of the time. In this state, we are comfortable and aware of our Core Self through our thoughts and feelings. We also have choices with what is fitting or relevant to share, depending on the company present.

Through an Honest Self state, we may also have a similar level of realness in terms of thoughts and a feeling of self-awareness; however, communication is more open and has less recognition for the potential impact on others. Though being an Honest Self may be optimal much of the time, there are times when social consideration and verbal constraint may be necessary.

Investigating Your Core Self

The goal of this model is to understand and accept our Core Self. Below are essential areas for us to explore so we may gain improved clarity about who we are as our Core Self. Ultimately, we want to understand our temperament and discover our inner true nature. Through this we may achieve a heightened level of positive acceptance for ourselves and others.

We can learn to get back to our Core Self through psychosocial insights and personal introspection. Through examining the following Sections I–V, we can investigate the areas that bring us closer to self-understanding. Through this process you should allow yourself the needed time it takes to honestly respond to the following questions and exercises.

Section I: Descriptors

We often internalize two dimensions of the Self. One is "how I see myself"; the other is my understanding of "how others see me." Sometimes these two aspects are similar, however other times there are differences.

Answer the following three questions with **descriptors** that best represent the image of who you are. You may identify physical attributes, special talents, skills, personality traits, or other self-features; choose descriptors that stand out the most. They are the significant characteristics that describe you from the perspectives of yourself and others. The number of descriptors for each question can vary.

1. How do I see myself?

_____

_____

_____

2. How do I think others see me?

_____

_____

_____

3. How do I want others to see me?

_____

_____

_____

- Differences between descriptors for each of the questions 1, 2, and 3 may reveal a different public persona compared to how one truly views themself or how they want to be seen.
- If there are similarities between the items in numbers 1 and 3, there is some congruence of the Self. How I see myself is actually how I want to be seen.
- If items 1, 2, and 3 appear similar, we are closest to our Core Self. This can be seen through a Real or Honest Self presentation.

Based on the descriptors you have documented in questions 1–3, try to describe yourself in a short yet meaningful sentence to illustrate yourself as your Real Self.

I am _____

_____

_____

Section II: Roles

There are many roles we manage throughout the day as well as roles we carry in the company of certain people in our lives. Do your best to identify as many roles as you can for yourself. Circle any role titles below that apply to you. There are also blank spaces for you to fill in for self-roles not listed. (You may include certain roles of your past if they are significant to you.)

Mother	Daughter	Nephew	Supervisor
Father	Best Friend	Cousin	Coach
Parent	Acquaintance	Historian	Musician
Stepparent	Grandmother	Photographer	Dancer
Sister	Grandfather	Teacher	Mentor
Brother	Grandson	Boyfriend	Athlete
Sibling	Granddaughter	Girlfriend	Neighbor
Husband	Godparent	Elder	Artist
Wife	Godchild	Guardian	Business Owner
Partner	Student	Employee	Retiree
Spouse	Aunt	Volunteer	Leader
Child	Uncle	Activist	Homemaker
Son	Niece	Writer	Church Member

Job Title _____ Expert on _____ Leader of _____

Others: _____

Others: _____

When you review this list of your roles, you will realize that some roles are a regular part of your routine life, while others will appear less frequently. It may be interesting to order these roles, starting from the ones occupying most of your time, down to your least active role.

1. _____   7. _____

2. _____   8. _____

3. _____   9. _____

4. _____   10. _____

5. _____   11. _____

6. _____   12. _____

You may then use the pie chart below to fill in your roles by their approximate percentage size. This will be the amount of time you express each role in your life.

Pie chart of time spent in each role.

While examining your many identified roles, which one(s) is/are most comfortable? In other words, which role(s) is/are experienced as most pleasant and genuine?

1. _____   3. _____

2. _____   4. _____

In a short sentence or two, try to express why this role(s) feels natural.

_____

_____

Section III: List and Examine Our Different Roles

Create a second listing of roles, but list only your most valued and personally meaningful ones. Write self-descriptors for each of the corresponding roles. There should be approximately two to three attributes best describing you for each role.

<u>Role</u>   <u>Self-Descriptors</u>

_____   _____

_____   _____

_____   _____

_____   _____

_____   _____

Search for any recurrent or similar self-descriptors appearing on the list above. If you find common attributes, write them in the grouping spaces on the next page.

If no common self-descriptors are noted between the different roles, try to look for some special commonality that might be shared between some or all of the roles. These will be new descriptors that were not initially written but could be relevant for the roles chosen.

Recurrent Self-Descriptors

First Grouping	Second Grouping	Third Grouping
_____	_____	_____
_____	_____	_____
_____	_____	_____
_____	_____	_____
_____	_____	_____

You may notice a common thread that is woven into all the roles you carry. These attributes may be consistently present and relate to your Core Self.

Write one to two brief sentences identifying and clarifying recognizable constants that are present within your most significant roles.

I am _____

_____

_____

Section IV: Core Self Understanding Through Temperament

Our personalities are made up of different elements (haecceity, temperament, traits, environmental factors) ranging from unchangeable to alterable. Though haecceity and temperament are always present as a constant in our lives, some of our traits may be modified, and our environmental factors, such as life experiences, may be altered by choice or by need. Combined, the four self-elements contribute to the development of an individual's personality.

Our deep essence influences our temperament. Though temperaments may be measurable, our internal nature is less definable. Haecceity is more of an abstract component of our intrinsic nature and is without a physical or concrete existence. It is an internal part of our Core Self, and we should not expect it to change.

Additionally, it is important that we acknowledge our own temperament style, since it is also a key component of our Core Self. Understanding temperament can be useful as a reference point for recognizing our inner nature. Temperament style is observable and is part of our Core Self. It operates as a function of the Core Self, influencing the way we approach the world when we are being more like our Real Self.

Within temperament types there are varying degrees of intensity for attributes. Traits can become qualitatively different for each individual. This is because we are all unique beings. Even within similar temperament types, differences are apparent.

Temperament has an effect on the way an individual is likely to behave in different life contexts. We are born with our temperament, which remains relatively steady into adulthood. It is our temperament that affects our social behavior and the way we engage within our environment. Ultimately, our interactions contribute to the development of our personality.

Temperament is a function of the mind that is relatively consistent over a person's lifespan, yet some of us actively or subconsciously try to adjust it. When altered, the associated thoughts, feelings, or behaviors may feel foreign and unnatural. When this happens, we may not feel balanced as our Core Self. Instead we may experience uncomfortable feelings of incongruity.

Since attributes of our temperament are present at birth, it may be interesting to examine how they have evolved over the years to our present. In the following exercise, try to explore some of the earliest memories of your self-temperament. These may be known through personal memory, what others have told you (parents, other elders, or friends) and/or observations from film/video/photographs. Early years may be determined as infant (0–1 year old), toddler (1–2 years), preschool (3–4 years), and school aged (5–12 years).

Take some time to recall past interactions with parents, siblings, family friends, teachers, peers, and others by exploring your temperament during your early years.

- What sort of feelings did I typically have in good times/bad times?
- Within positive and negative experiences, how did I communicate my emotions?
- What was my natural approach to new situations?

- Were there common ways I regulated my behavior, such as cooperating with others, taking turns, following rules, and adapting to new environments?

While reviewing memories of your early years, can you identify a time when you were most uninhibited and free to express yourself without negative concerns? These were times when your temperament was operating most naturally.

As we grow older, our temperament style may evolve into something different. This happens when we want to please other people or try to avoid negative consequences from them. Through this, we may disconnect with certain parts of our Core Self. Below are questions relating to your temperament to determine if there are changes from your original approach to others and situations. These questions are meant to increase your Core Self awareness.

1. Did my temperament style ever change to match the expectations of others?

    Yes No What age(s) did this happen?   Age(s) ____ ____ ____

    Oftentimes we adjust our natural approach to life (temperament), but it may be at the cost of feeling incongruent. Do I approach life circumstances differently than I did in my early years?

    Yes No If yes, how does this change feel?

    _____

    _____

    _____

2. What observable parts of my temperament did I have as a child that remain with me today when (if) presenting as a Real Self?

    _____

    _____

    _____

3. How would I guide myself as a child? How would I support and preserve that child's temperament?

_____

_____

_____

Section V: Reinforcing Personal Qualities

Each of us has unique qualities inherent to the Self. Acknowledging this brings us closer to a Real Self mentality, which can be freeing. Unfortunately, there may be external pressures to abandon parts of the Self and accept a system's mindset of different values and behaviors that are not your own. This can trigger emotional discomfort and uneasiness. The further we pull away from our Core Self, the more likely we will feel incongruity, which may lead to anxiousness and depressive symptoms.

7 Ways to Get Closer to Your Core Self

1. List the qualities of yourself that you can acknowledge as positive strengths. These are the qualities that help define you as an individual.

2. Try to process the elements of your temperament that have appeared consistent over time (from childhood to present). This may be achieved through personal insights as well as recalling emotional reactions to stressors, understanding how you engage people, and simply examining daily life activities.

3. Explore personal interests on your own. Approach these interests in your own way and in a way that helps you enjoy the process.

4. Allow yourself leisure time to relax and step away from external pressures. Time for yourself is a form of reclaiming your life by briefly stepping away from outside pressures. You get to choose how much time you need for yourself. This must be done guilt-free.

5. Journal your thoughts and feelings regarding new events and the people you are engaging. This may help you to focus on your Real Self. After this you may choose to explore how to express yourself socially.

6. Reflect on positive moments of the past, preferably your early child-hood. These were times you were most likely behaving as your Real or Honest Self.

7. Review some of the positive relationships from your life. These are people you feel most comfortable with to show your Real Self. Your Real Self is borne out of your Core Self.

Acknowledging our personal qualities and accepting them are two different things. We may have heard others remark on our nature and character. We may have even identified certain personal qualities on our own. However, we may not comfortably accept our qualities fully as a significant part of our identity.

Accepting yourself is the key to unlocking the block that prevents you from being authentic. If we are able to accept ourselves, we may also have the understanding and compassion to accept others.

8 Ways to Embrace and Accept Your Core Self

1. Allow yourself alone time. Being by yourself can be contemplative. It allows you time to reflect on your own inner nature.

2. Replace negative self-thoughts with realistic self-statements to reinforce what you already know about yourself.

3. Question or challenge outside expectations placed on you when they do not match who you are as a Real Self.

4. Associate more with the people who are accepting of you. Be with those who can see you for who you are and will not try to change you. Mutual acceptance between you and others is a good thing.

5. Know that it is reasonable to accept support from others. Genuine support simply means someone cares and is willing to offer you what you need in a concerned and understanding way. These are not people who manipulate or push an opinion. They may know elements of your Core Self and may know what you need at a particular time. Accept a cooperative connection with others.

6. Concentrate on who **you** are instead of "what others think you are" or "what others want you to be."

7. Know your strengths and weaknesses, and try to embrace the areas worth improving.

8. Utilize psychotherapy as a means of gaining deeper Core Self insights and to improve self-congruity.

Chapter Summary

In this chapter we have explored several ways to understand different parts of our Core Self. Through these practices, we should become more aware of a deeper part within ourselves. Using the exercises offered, we may increase our insights and be better aligned with the uniquenesses we all possess. In Core Self Theory, there is a Core Self that is unique and separate from all other individuals. It's something more internal and spiritual rather than being simply about genetics.

The Core Self is the part of the Self that has always existed and is always with us. The Real and Honest Self may share similarities since they are positively influenced by the Core Self. Life history and other life circumstances can also influence our development. Ultimately, I can recognize who I am as a Core Self and behave as a Real or Honest Self.

In Sections I, II, and III, there are exercises meant to increase your awareness about your Core Self. Each of these sections also conclude with personal self-statements. These self-statements may be used as a tool to help you get closer to your Core Self. These are used similarly to cognitive restructuring techniques (such as changing negative thoughts to more realistic ones). They can be used as realistic Core Self mantras reminding yourself of who you are, rather than presenting a different self that is not consistent with your Core Self.

These self-statements may be said internally and repeated as a reminder of your Core Self qualities. Knowing the mantras by memory and saying them routinely can reinforce Core Self thoughts and feelings. It should also bring you comfortably closer to being more of a Real or Honest Self. Less incongruity of the Self should also help decrease anxiety or depressive symptoms.

This process can help decrease negative thoughts and aid you to become more realistic and positive. Negative thoughts interfere with self-acceptance. Cognitive restructuring techniques can help change unuseful thinking to something more realistic or positive.

Section IV is intended as a reflection overview on earlier parts of your past. This was a time when you felt more freedom to be yourself, and you were less aware of judgments from others. This section focuses on the progression of your temperament that may have been edited to the point of your feeling incongruent. Any insights related to you-then and you-now can be processed personally. Psychotherapy may also be beneficial for working on temperament changes in greater depth.

Finally, Section V tries to reinforce what is necessary to approach your Core Self qualities. There are certain ways you can get closer to your Core Self, but embracing the deeper parts of yourself is critical. This is where you are challenged to accept your Core Self and move closer to accepting others.

Chapter 9

Core Self Theory in Therapy

This chapter explores the application of Core Self Theory in a therapeutic setting. The chosen cases aid as examples to describe treatment. They are meant for the purpose of demonstrating the benefits of this model when engaged with clients through the practice of psychotherapy. The example cases illustrate the factors to take into consideration when a therapist approaches a client through issues primarily related to depression and anxiety. The method is supportive and pulls for emotional affect to help a client get in touch with their Real Self. This approach also increases self-awareness and self-acceptance.

This form of therapy aims to engage and appreciate personal elements of the Core Self. It supports positive openness for the client, helping them release fears of being negatively criticized or judged. Through this, clients may gain a greater understanding of who they are, as they strive to embrace self-acceptance.

The finest statement I have found relating to this concept of self-acceptance comes from the Humanistic Psychologist Carl Rogers, who wrote, "The curious paradox is that when I accept myself just as I am, then I can change" (*On Becoming a Person: A Therapist's View of Psychotherapy*, 1961). Here, the message is that growth comes when we accept who we are rather than merely focusing on self-improvement. This also includes accepting our positive and negative traits. Through this self-acceptance, we may then have the capacity to grow. As we grow to like our inner selves, self-confidence increases and opens us to new possibilities.

The initial goal of this therapy is to acknowledge and understand one's Core Self. The other objectives are embracing the inner self as we are, as well as being open and welcoming toward others. Behavioral edits of the Self may also be examined but are superfluous in this early stage of exploration. It is the processing of our Core Self that is initially important, since that part of ourselves is experienced best when it is real, stable, and consistent. Any behavioral changes we make are best when they are made for positive purposes, such as improving communication approaches with others.

Recognizing and appreciating the Core Self is useful. It advances deeper insight through understanding and valuing who a person really is from past to present. Exploring the deepest parts of the Core Self may be thought of as something more innate, such as with haecceity and temperament. Other components of the Self relate to traits, which may also have existed at birth, and environmental factors, which include such things as cultural background, life circumstances, and social interactions. From the perspective of our possessing these four personality elements, it is essential that we know which ones may be modified.

- Haecceity is our deepest part of the Self, our true essence. It is assumed to be unchangeable. It is a quality that may be undefinable and yet uniquely separates us from all other individuals.

- Temperament, as another Core Self element, is also considered unchangeable and is part of the Self that was present at birth. While less abstract than one's haecceity, it is more recognizable and definable. When we try to explore a person's temperament, we are usually able to put words to their particular Self type or nature. It is a disposition that is present and felt by an individual and noticed by others. When it is unchanged and consistently experienced by others, it suggests that the individual is somewhat comfortable behaving as their Real or Honest Self.

- Traits, however, are numerous and may be influenced by temperament. They may be felt and expressed naturally or may be altered when transformed by internal or external elements.

- Lastly, environmental factors can interplay with traits and temperament. Depending on the type of factor impacting the Self, positive or negative reactions will follow. With consistent consequences that follow, the environment may shape the individual, thus pulling them away from their true Core Self. Over time, it may be hard to discern what is the Real Self and what is not.

Personality Elements, from unchanging to alterable:

Combined, the above elements of the Self result in an individual's personality. Recognize that we are born with a certain haecceity and temperament. Our internal essence influences our temperament and traits, which are measurable and definable. Haecceity, however, is something that is more intangible and abstract. It is an internal part of each individual's life, and we should not expect it to change. Additionally, temperament is an attitude of the mind that also does not truly change, yet we may actively or subconsciously attempt to modify it. When altered, the associated thoughts, feelings, or behaviors that come from a temperament style may feel foreign and unnatural. When this occurs, we are imbalanced and not our Real Self. At these junctures of life we may feel uncomfortable states of incongruity.

Certain behavioral changes may edit the presentation of a temperament style. Changes in our temperament lead to shifts with how we manage traits. If we recognize that traits are influenced by our temperament, altering temperament should reshape certain trait features, thus changing the presentation of our personalities. Traits may then have the capacity to change, depending on their type. Central traits are most likely affected. They are generally common characteristics that are found in most of us at varying degrees. They are considered the parts of our personality that are especially significant. Common central trait examples include such qualities as jealousy, assertiveness, loyalty, honesty, dependability, and kindness.

Ultimately, a change in thought and behavior can eventually change how we manage and present our traits. It can also change a feeling. What should have been expressed as something natural becomes edited to fit a new paradigm related to the new self-state. This format is probably more pleasing to others, yet feels unnatural and incongruent to the changed Self. Repetitive alterations that vary from self-congruousness will change a person's safe and comfortable need for Core Self acceptance. Incongruity of Self prevents a natural progression toward self-acceptance. A key objective of therapy is to then identify the progression of change leading a person from a place of Real Self congruency to the incongruence felt by becoming a Lost or Hidden Self.

A summary of the progression from the Core Self to a state of incongruity is illustrated below:

- Core Self comfort experienced from being real.

- Person experiences negative consequences/admonishment from authority figures or dominant groups when behaving as their Core Self.

- Person tries to modify behavior/communication to resort to a safer Lost or Hidden Self.

- Temperament is managed differently than before. A person changes their general life approach to fit in with others' expectations.

- Affected temperament influences how traits are now handled.

- Traits are altered to fit with a change in temperament style.

- Personality is edited and becomes distant from the Real or Honest Self.

- Emotional discomfort is felt at varying degrees, depending on how much difference exists between the Core Self and current self-state (Lost, Hidden, Real, and Honest Self).

A productive focus is on self-acceptance while also recognizing we may have gone astray from our Core Self due to various life experiences and social influences. It is best to hone in on the factors that are incongruent with our Core Self and work toward realignment. Also, understand that parts of personality and state of mind are constant and unchangeable (such as haecceity), while other parts are changeable. The important aspect of this is to know which is which from within ourselves. It actually comes down to an age-old question of nature versus nurture. The Core Self may be considered part nature and somewhat spiritual, since it is more of who we are and always were. The social and environmental factors fall more on the side of nurture, since it is what we have experienced in the world that influences us.

Nature versus nurture is an established discussion in science regarding different facets of life that determine one's fate: biology/genetics versus the influence of environmental factors. Nature relates best to the idea of one's quiddity/haecceity and our natural-born temperament, since it appears without social influence and is carried with us throughout our lives. A person's traits may also be considered part of the nature side, since we are born with a unique genetic combination of traits; however, environmental factors may also influence certain traits.

Since nurture is concerned with outside influences or external factors, changes related to one's temperament can affect the way traits get shaped by the environment. Recognizing a client's struggle with their nurture experiences (environmental factors) and how their experiences impact their nature sets the focus of treatment. Through this understanding, we can aid clients in becoming reacquainted with their Core Self after identifying the life experiences that have impacted them.

One of the best approaches to getting to know our Real Self is examining earliest memories. Besides the recall of important life events, we will also want to remember what we felt and how we behaved. When this is not easily accomplished due to poor memory, blocked recall, or difficulty processing the feelings with behavior, we can ask others we trust. They may have stories in our past history that can help us decipher the Self.

Through the help of a therapist, one can also explore emotional reactions to significant life events (positive and negative) by helping them uncover and reveal the inner feelings that may be guarded for emotional safety. What follows is an exploration relating to a deciphering of incongruent experiences that do not align with the Core Self. By identifying these unnatural changes in the Self, the client can learn to make sense of their emotional discomfort that may have led them to experiencing feelings of anxiety and depression.

Examples of Cases

What follows are sample cases of individuals who have explored their own levels of incongruity compared to their Core Self. These shared cases are meant to illustrate common struggles that we may experience when we drift away from who we really are. Most of these individuals entered therapy because they were feeling unhappy. Their goals related to changes that would improve self-esteem and improve appropriate assertiveness. Aside from a general counseling approach that is meant to guide a person in achieving or getting something in the future, a psychotherapy approach was necessary to acquire a deeper understanding of the Self. Psychotherapy empowers a client to explore significant life experiences from the past. Many of these experiences relate to changes that alter the Core Self.

The individuals discussed in the following vignettes are not specifically identified and some are composites of clients. Their names are changed and any other identifying features are altered.

Reclaiming a Positive Self-Image

Sarah was a thirty-one-year-old female who came in for treatment to work on chronic feelings of depression. She had seen a therapist for two years prior and was feeling stuck due to marginal changes or progress with her general mood. Though she did feel she gained some positive benefits within her previous therapy, such as learning increased social engagement and developing healthier daily routines, she wanted to process her feelings with the goal of improving her mood, engaging others more comfortably, and gaining a deeper understanding of her inner self with self-acceptance. Her symptoms included sadness, low motivation, irregular sleep pattern, poor concentration, and a general sense of apathy with low interest in the activities she had once enjoyed. Though medication was recommended by her previous therapist, she felt uncomfortable trying medication at this stage of her treatment.

Following her intake, which explored her history of depression, we discussed her personal goals that she felt were important and could be the focus of treatment. Sarah's primary interest was centered on issues of low self-esteem. She identified herself as someone who tries hard but struggles with feeling successful or not being good enough. This theme permeated her life in ways that affected her within her family of origin, her relationships, and her sense of herself at work. Other self-descriptors included feeling awkward, worthless, ineffective, and avoidant. Beyond these negative Self views, it was difficult to verbalize positive descriptors for herself.

At this point, Sarah was asked how she believed others thought of her. This too was challenging, considering all of her efforts were directed to the negative self-image she believed was seen by others. It was realistic for her to accept that she carried positive traits. She was encouraged to share and verbalize them. Positive traits were expressed and related to her general character, such as being trustworthy, caring about others, and being diligent about her responsibilities.

In her following sessions, Sarah was able to explore elements of her Core Self and recall times in her life when she felt more secure and did not struggle with the issue of self-acceptance. As expected, Sarah recalled positive feelings from early childhood, playing among her friends in the neighborhood. She remembered her feelings and stated she had felt positive and genuinely good about herself. This exploration of the past was important, since it allowed her to separate her current feelings with real feelings of the past. Here, it was important to remind Sarah that the young child she remembered was still her. The person is the same but existing at different periods of her life. The differences between then and now are the negative influences that may have taken away freedoms that were more permissible as a youngster. As a child, she was comfortable being herself and was unaware of criticisms or judgments from others.

The judgments felt by most of us may simply be directives and shaping from authority figures. These well-intentioned people may include our parents, grandparents, teachers, coaches, and parents of friends. Sometimes their only goal is to keep order and peace, however the end result may be an editing of the joy that comes from free expressiveness. For some individuals, the guidance is mild with low to moderate negative effects. For others, the direction can be stronger. It is hard to determine the level of an individual's experience when they are pressured to change thoughts, feelings, or actions. Usually, this sort of experience is progressive and adds up over time. However, the way it is communicated can shed light on who the significant influences were and what their message was about expressing an Honest Self.

For Sarah, there was recall of being told her playing was too tomboyish and her behavior was too controlling and aggressive. Some might see Sarah's behavior as assertive and possessing leadership qualities. But in this case, she was directed to behave in ways that were considered more feminine and "ladylike." Through repeated punitive statements meant to change Sarah's free-flowing, natural behavior, she was discouraged enough to alter parts of her Core Self.

Similar shaping by others seemed to continue from childhood to her current adult status. Sarah had altered her Core Self and managed to comply with the expectations of others to the point of changing who she was. This change of Self became an internal problem for Sarah, but externally, it seemed to help her by minimizing arguments and other social difficulties. Her compliance appeared as cooperativeness, which made others happy.

Sarah often felt frustrated with inner conflict. She could not easily identify the source of her emotional problems; however, she did not feel good about herself and found it difficult to connect with others. Through processing her related feelings of anxiousness and depression, we were able to identify the part of herself that felt disconnected to her deeper Self. We were able to define Sarah's temperament. It was that part of her that was present from her earliest stages of life. It was observable as a young daughter, sibling, student, and friend. If properly embraced, it could have remained with her throughout her life. Without the ideal support to be her Real Self, Sarah was challenged to reclaim the unmodified Self from her past.

Sarah's success with this treatment came through the acknowledgment of her Core Self and feeling safe enough to think, feel, and behave in ways that came naturally. She also found self-acceptance, which ultimately enabled her to be more comfortable engaging others as her Honest Self. With these few but significant changes, Sarah felt more relaxed, with decreased anxiety. Her mood became generally pleasant and less depressed. She was not as guarded as before. Natural instincts began emerging, and genuine reactions appeared. Sarah chose to return to that earlier version of herself, the Self who was uninhibited and free. With this level of openness, she was aware of herself and not a Lost or Hidden Self.

Core Self Deviation

Maggie is a middle-aged woman with a family consisting of two children and her husband. She entered into therapy to work on issues that consisted of anxiousness in social situations and mild depression. After working several months in individual therapy, Maggie shared that her social communication is usually very verbal, and she tended to appear extroverted within various social groups. However, the anticipation of social interactions created feelings of self-doubt and anxiety. Just thinking about social interactions triggered a type of panic accompanied by a negative view of herself. Mentally preparing for gatherings and functions felt exhausting. The other important problem she identified related to a struggle to connect with other females. She stated that she was "afraid of women."

Given Maggie's history with females, growing up with a mother and sisters who constantly argued dramatically, I reframed her disclosure as "It's less about being afraid of women; it's your background history of female conflicts creating that feeling." She agreed to explore the possibility of my assumption and eventually recognized that when she was very young, she did not fear women (her natural Core Self). She stated, "I actually loved being around women and other girls." Her "fear" seemed to develop out of the environment she grew up in. Whether it was triggered by her mother and sisters or some other significant women (such as female teachers), it eventually developed into what she called "a fear of women." This was important because we could go back and therapeutically acknowledge her Core Self at an early age. We identified her temperament as easygoing and trusting toward others, and saw that she did not specifically demonstrate or feel a fear of women.

Through exploring her open and pleasant presentation as a child, Maggie actually recalled stories with examples of enjoying the company of women and other girls. Over time, those interactions were eventually shaped into something outside of what her Core Self initially experienced. What started out as purely positive feelings with high levels of trust resulted in a life journey that became negative and mistrusting of women in general. Interestingly, as an adult woman, her Core Self was naturally drawn to engage in meaningful connections with other women, both professionally and socially. She often described the desire to have a female best friend, or at least a friend she could trust. However, this was difficult to achieve, considering most of her friendships felt competitive and punitive with an overwhelming feeling of rejection.

Much of Maggie's history came from the way she was raised and the presence of significant females who were negative in her life. The conundrum was that she was drawn to connect with women in meaningful ways, while personal life experiences created anxiety and drew her away from most female relationships. By helping Maggie recognize her Core Self comfort as a child, around other females, she was able to discover that only a few life experiences and certain significant people affected her subconscious fears of women. Through this recognition, and aiming to behave more as her Real Self, she was able to slowly work toward better communication with women and feel improved comfort with these actions.

In a later session, Maggie shared a related issue and an example of her discomfort and mistrust of certain women. She was recently stuck in a work situation that took her out of her calm and diplomatic emotional place and ended with stern, confrontational statements. This occurred after a female coworker repeatedly manipulated and verbally pushed Maggie, which eventually caused her to change her approach. When she addressed this conflict in therapy, she felt bad about herself. She worked hard to be professional yet felt forced to do something she "did not want to do." It was not in her nature. Sometimes we feel we "have to do" things we do not want to do. The need to behave assertively was an appropriate choice given the circumstances; however, Maggie stepped out of her Core Self, which was atypical and felt unnatural.

The incident was processed as being an occurrence that precipitated incongruent feelings that did not relate to her Core Self. Maggie liked to make people happy. She also avoided conflicts. For her to cross the line beyond her comfort zone of peaceful exchanges with others, especially women, was significant. When this was discussed, she struggled to see her own good nature and assumed the negative behavior was actually reflective of her Core Self. Instead, it appeared that her communication change was the breaking point that required assertiveness. Maggie was stern and labeled what she was seeing; she was not loud, hurtful, or aggressive. She was able to state the facts but with a different, more serious tone.

The consideration to observe in this scenario is that we may be drawn into situations requiring interventions that are not part of our temperament or approach to life stressors. However, there are times when we can feel required to intervene when assertiveness takes precedence. Knowing this should be useful. Even when it feels incongruent, it can be a useful choice that feels better than resorting to unwanted compliance to avoid conflict. Maggie was her Real Self, yet she temporarily made a detour that felt out of sync but kept her empowered. She was still the same Maggie, only she made a necessary response that pulled for other traits that were not as comfortable to her Real Self.

Childhood Assertiveness

A similar example of Core Self incongruence relates to a middle school boy who entered therapy due to his parents' concern over recent episodes of anxiety and depression. Mitchell, a nine-year-old boy, experienced peer bullying and was uncomfortable addressing the issue directly. His father wanted him to confront his bully peers when provoked, though such behavior was not his real nature.

Mitchell presented with a quiet and pleasant attitude. He looked happy most of the time, especially when playing outside with other classmates or neighborhood children. Mitchell never intended to hurt other people's feelings and was genuinely surprised that another peer would criticize him or mock him for minor things that were part of his character. Under these conditions, Mitchell was becoming sad and depressed. He began displaying signs of anxiety through school avoidance and a growing social phobia. He was being harassed, which made him question his comfort with his Core Self identity.

Addressing this issue was somewhat sensitive, but the problems would likely persist without a clear intervention. Seeing that Mitchell's temperament was nonaggressive and that he actively chose not to engage in conflicts, it was important to utilize a Goodness of Fit approach to help his parents view the problem through Mitchell's eyes. Mitchell's Core Self might be at risk for being dismissed if he were to be pushed into an attack mode, since this was not his true nature. Therefore, a clear reminder for the parents to remember who their son is, and how his temperament has always been, was a positive joining moment for the family. It was also important to recognize and support the father's interest in teaching Mitchell limit-setting skills when dealing with peers who were harassing him. Without learning this behavior, Mitchell might carry an unwanted identity, placing him in a victim role.

Aside from receiving the needed support and understanding from his parents, Mitchell also processed his discomfort in confronting his bully peers. To move past this barrier, the next step in therapy was to explore his own ability to assert himself in nonconfrontational situations. This was beneficial since it opened up his own recognition that in the past he had behaved assertively and experienced positive outcomes. After this recognition, Mitchell became more open to practice assertiveness in other situations. Assertiveness no longer equated to his old belief that it was an attitude of aggression. Instead, assertiveness was a trait with personal skills, allowing him to verbalize his thoughts with stated facts over what was not appropriate or acceptable from his bully peers.

Through this particular case, the child was initially resistant to changing his behavior since assertiveness felt out of character and he was afraid of a potential negative outcome. Parental support certainly played an important role with his change. It was clear that Mitchell's temperament was not aggressive, and so he was not encouraged or pushed to behave differently from his inner nature. However, certain actions were necessary for him to address the bullying and move forward.

The skill of assertiveness does not require that someone change who they are but can feel out of character when one's nature is to get along and cooperate with others in a genuinely positive way. The resolution to Mitchell's problem resulted in one or two verbal exchanges that ultimately fizzled out into no further bullying. The growth for this child was significant and promoted self-acceptance along with newly added assertiveness tools that can be used at times when setting limits is most appropriate.

Squabble at the PTA

Returning to our Core Self is a process and not an event. It means that over time we become aware of who we are, accept it, and then work with it. The advantage of behaving as our Core Self is that we become better acquainted with our own true thoughts and feelings. With this profound level of self-understanding, we can decide when to act as our best and most authentic version of ourselves. Conscious awareness and self-acceptance lead to both personal choices and individualized behaviors that are congruent with our Core Self. Through this, we have the opportunity to choose to be a Hidden, Real, or Honest Self.

Being the Hidden Self as a routine option is not the healthiest version of the Self, but it does have its place under certain situations. It may be properly utilized during times of stress, while still implying an inner awareness of the Core Self. Under such circumstances, the negative emotions related to incongruence are uncomfortably accepted while certain thoughts, feelings, and values are concealed. The complication with this choice is that the Hidden Self is playing a role that is not aligned with the Core Self. This may create negative feelings within oneself.

Behaving as a Real or Honest Self should always be considered as an ideal, however these may not always require complete openness when presented with uniquely difficult circumstances. Life sometimes presents us with situations that carry low significance and do not require a firm emotional investment with our Real or Honest Self. At times we may maintain Real Self thoughts and feelings, but we are not required to fully verbalize or act on them. As long as we are not compromising personal values or behaving in ways contrary to our Core Self, we can choose behaviors that are more diplomatic. In some situations, it is best to merely retain the knowledge of who we are and what we believe in, rather than to go down the path of asserting ourselves unnecessarily to others.

An example relates to Cynthia, who described conflictual issues with another woman at her children's school Parent Teacher Association (PTA). The woman provoked Cynthia in such a way that it became obvious to other parents that there was a problem. The woman was somewhat two-faced and worked behind the scenes to include other women to back up her hostile agenda. In part, her intentions included delegitimizing Cynthia's positions in leadership and trying to oust her from her leadership roles. This seemed to stem from the woman's jealousy toward Cynthia. The woman also lacked the ability to join people together. Instead of trying to work harmoniously, she divided in order to conquer.

In therapy, Cynthia asked the question, "How do I respond to this woman when she approaches me with a smile and asks me how things are going?" which seemed to happen routinely. This question was interesting because it placed Cynthia in a position of internal conflict. Cynthia did not like trouble, but she also had a strong assertive side that wanted to address issues and conflicts that involved her. On one side, Cynthia could be her Honest Self and confront the woman's nonsensical and manipulative behavior by calling her out with a nonaggressive tone. This would be expressed through making factual, yet negatively provoking statements. Another option was for Cynthia to keep her inner thoughts to herself, while still operating as an aware Real Self.

This Real Self option was a better choice, since she was internally clear about her own personal thoughts and feelings as well as being in control of her outward behavior. Through deeper analysis, we can recognize she was not obligated to share what she wanted to express, since the end result would create more negativity within the community that they share. It would also perpetuate the socially dysfunctional relationship between Cynthia and the woman. It could increase the likelihood of further fueling the divisiveness factor that was already started. In this situation, having the insight about the problem and choosing to manage the communication, with a semi-comfortable tone, resulted in a peaceful exchange that did not compromise Cynthia's need to be her Core Self.

Oftentimes it becomes a natural reflex to know what is beneficial to withhold from the public or even those who are socially close. Would you consider an Honest Self presentation through revealing personal opinions if they might create anger, hurt, or confusion for the recipients of your communication? Withholding an honest viewpoint that creates negativity might be best handled conscientiously and diplomatically. Honesty may not always be the best policy, yet being consciously aware of your intention, with accurate self-understanding, permits us to make choices with what we express. The Real Self is important in this situation, since we are aware of our own thoughts and feelings. Real Self behavior simply means we are in touch with our Core Self and can make conscious decisions about how we interact with certain others within various contexts.

Dancing for Real

In a similar example within a therapy setting, a young woman named Joanna shared that she was experiencing a personal transformation in the way she interacted with others. She grew up learning gymnastics but eventually became a trained theater dancer. She previously viewed herself as an introvert who developed into an extroverted person due to her experience as a dancer. In reality, her earlier years were focused on gymnastic practices and competitions.

She recalled being "in my head" and took her sport seriously. Joanna pulled away from her natural tendency to run around and play as most children do. Instead, she was absorbed with her activities and wanted to make her parents proud. She was more of a loner at school and did not make many friends through her gymnastics team. In fact, within that group of peers, she experienced less support and more competitiveness.

Eventually, Joanna found her Real Self through the expressive art of dance. Previously, she was operating as a Hidden Self until she discovered that revealing herself gave her greater comfort. This change felt so dramatic that she also became more verbally open and uninhibited, letting her Honest Self emerge. To some, her new behavior was unwanted. She was sharing thoughts and ideas that were not always popular.

However, when Joanna felt free to act as her Honest Self, she was unreserved, verbally engaged, and genuinely happy with self-confidence. This was positive, yet with this level of openness and freedom, she realized others were less comfortable with her. The feedback she subtly received was sometimes negative or passive-aggressive. Though this felt punitive, Joanna would not allow herself to feel insecurities over the judgments of other people.

Commonly, her peers behaved as if they did not understand her. Some even avoided her. Over time, she was bothered enough that she decided to decrease her style of openness. This was a calculated choice. Joanna backed off from being routinely spontaneous and uninhibited. She selectively edited how she conveyed thoughts and feelings and to whom.

Being shunned or discouraged from being her Honest Self was not a pleasant feeling. Instead, she chose to limit her Honest Self, even though she preferred the freedom experienced from open expression. Joanna felt a need to censor her Honest Self and began realizing there were aspects of herself that others did not want to know or understand. She began choosing when it was comfortable to be her Honest Self but would always remain her Real Self.

This decision to partially withdraw from total free expression seemed unfortunate but did not make Joanna sad. She remained aware of her Real Self yet knew what to share and with whom. Her comfort came from both verbal and nonverbal expressiveness. She could emote in whatever style of communication she chose, such as with dance. Her decision to remain her Real Self and limit her Honest Self expression was a conscious one. Her approach toward others had limitations, but she was able to choose to interact with the type of people who fit her personality best. She would be herself in the presence of others who encouraged the openness she loved to share. This was learned from personal past experiences and the reactions from those with whom she engaged. In the end, she was her Core Self.

Reclaiming the Core Self

Awareness of the Core Self can be accomplished through therapeutic insights. This may be achieved when a client is open in therapy and verbalizes what is truly felt. For some, recognizing Lost Self behavior as a problem may be a first step for the client's movement toward improved mental health. The Lost Self is considered furthest from being a Real or Honest Self and can therefore create a significant incongruence with the Self. A Lost Self position in life may be difficult to acknowledge; however, it can also motivate a client to want to understand their Core Self and start to be real.

In therapy a client stated, "I am doing well but a little anxious." Robert was a seventeen-year-old male client who shared his personal insight about how he frequently carried a role as a peacemaker. He also had a tendency to please others while putting his own needs last. This led to his awareness of how past childhood experiences in his family contributed to his inclination to resolve conflicts between others, outside the family. Robert reduced the occurrences of negative escalations by making peace. He also strived to feel acceptance externally by behaving as a helper for others.

As a child, Robert grew up witnessing family arguments and domestic violence. These were past traumatic events that created his triggers for feeling anxiousness and a strong sense of cautiousness. Robert tried to play the role of peacemaker within his family. This ultimately led to behaviors meant to keep a calm atmosphere while trying to care for other people's needs. He sought out peace and safety, actively focusing on how he could create positive surroundings for the people with whom he engaged. He stated, "If I don't please people, I'll get rejected and feel worthless around my peers."

Much of Robert's awareness came from a sustained negative self-image. This negative view of himself was reinforced by hostile peers who were judgmental and critical. At times he felt like an outsider, so he learned to adapt to his environment as well as the people he encountered. He eventually realized he was behaving as a Lost Self, since much of his behavior came outside of what he naturally felt and wanted to do. His actions became more of a reflex that was subconsciously driven. He had an automatic response to conflict or acted with a preemptive strike to avoid situations that carried the potential for negative outcomes.

At that time in therapy, he recognized that his traumatic childhood was the primary source of his anxious feelings and that it impacted him throughout his life. He avoided conflicts, disagreements, and arguments rather than questioning others and being assertive. Early experiences taught him to lighten the mood rather than address it honestly. His childhood anxiety of things getting out of control actually created his inner conflict that developed into anxiety based on self-incongruence.

In therapy, Robert was willing to explore his Core Self. He tried to understand his early childhood temperament along with the characteristics that may have helped him cope. He had traits related to caring for others as well as the courage to intervene and help them in times of crisis. These traits however could have been expressed in better ways, through being positively influenced by his Core Self temperament. Instead he was lost and anxious, trying to manage other people's negativity for the sake of peace. Unfortunately, he veered away from his more Real or Honest Self. Ideally, Robert could have asserted his true feelings and maintained what was genuinely felt as a youth to carry through to his childhood and into late adolescence.

Robert's therapy insight was valuable. He recognized an incongruent set of behaviors that were out of sync with his Core Self. After processing his thoughts and feelings from earlier life experiences, Robert was more open to seeing how his temperament made a shift from what was initially easygoing to a style of being frustrated and anxious. Instead of naturally engaging others with openness, honesty, and a general concern for Self and others, he developed additional traits that showed him to be rigid and guarded, with more concern for others than himself. Embracing his natural Core Self tendencies, rather than false ones, meant he could start behaving more as his Real or Honest Self. He could also accept that most social interactions can be safe. His role no longer carried a responsibility of keeping others comfortable. Instead, he could share his thoughts while being mindful of others' feelings yet not neglecting his own.

Not Following the Crowd

Behaving as one's Core Self as a young child may initially feel safe and comfortable. At that time, being oneself is all that is really known. As children get older, they begin to understand the costs and benefits of operating as a Real or Honest Self. Maintaining their natural Core Self may progressively become more challenging. For some, it is less demanding to cooperate and get along with social expectations. This would include certain standards of what is considered acceptable group behavior.

For others, it is particularly difficult to feign such allegiance. For those who stay true to their Core Self without suffering negative consequences from the outside, their lives will likely continue with a higher probability of stability and congruence. For others who actively preserved and continued their Core Self but received minimal support, their life struggles may be greater. For this category of people, difficulties may persist until actively processed, with a movement toward changing back to a Real Self presentation.

Being our consistent Real Self can be demanding, especially when outside verbal and nonverbal cues give us negative feedback. This may be seen with the client Jennifer, who was a forty-two-year-old married mother of two children. In therapy, she questioned and strived to understand why she seemingly could not connect adequately with others. Though she was described as an extrovert and was well liked by most people, she historically had a limited ability to join closer to others as well as maintain long-lasting friendships.

Jennifer questioned whether she had some sort of subconscious issue preventing her from communicating effectively. Socially, she presented fine. She was also a clear and kind communicator. However, a subtle yet noticeable behavior of Jennifer related to her own dismissal of other people. She seemed to have a limited ability to engage in what she termed "nonsense talk" and did not enjoy discussions that were unstimulating. These included conversations such as small talk, gossip, and dwelling on unimportant stories that were shared for the umpteenth time.

It was revealed in therapy that Jennifer had difficulty playing politics and behaving diplomatically. Historically, she had never satisfactorily played expected roles among her peers. She also did not strive to join them socially or get along in ways that could connect her better, which could possibly allow friendships to flourish. Instead, she wanted freedom to think and act as she chose. Even as a child, she was most comfortable speaking her mind, even at the cost of alienating peers or getting in trouble with adult authority figures. She believed most of her peers behaved predictably, in terms of group expectations. This was behavior that was unfamiliar to Jennifer. Her tendency was to be her Real or Honest Self rather than being accepted by a group as a Lost or Hidden Self.

If we look back and examine Jennifer's youth, we see she grew up in a small town where she attended the local public schools. She described herself as frequently feeling alone, wandering around the schoolyard and not feeling part of any group. She felt a sense of embarrassment and hid her feelings of aloneness, hoping the other children would not notice she was not connected to any particular group. Through her own insight into these behaviors, it was clear that she was not comfortable playing roles or acting as if she was part of any group where she could not be herself. The unfortunate side to these Core Self behaviors was that she was often alone, yet she really wanted to engage others.

Jennifer's problem was not that she behaved as her Core Self. Her issues stemmed more from not knowing better diplomatic skills to get along with others. She would have also benefited from recognizing her own limits of tolerance with those she could not connect with. Through these skills, Jennifer would hypothetically maintain her Real Self while managing personal limits with her Honest Self.

At some point she developed a connection with a peer from grammar school. Her friend Victoria was an introverted girl who frequently sat alone at lunchtime. Eventually, Jennifer began a friendship with this girl who had felt alienated by her peers. She was able to connect with Victoria in a way that did not compromise her own thoughts, feelings, or beliefs. She was also very accepting of Victoria, which made their friendship simple and unconditional. With this, she was true to her Core Self.

This recall of her grammar school friend was important since it reminded Jennifer that she was capable of developing friendships, even though they were few in number. Jennifer realized she had her own limits with what felt comfortable when communicating to others. She also remembered past decision making that helped her maintain her Core Self. This meant she was herself in social situations, which was positive. It also meant that she commonly avoided joining peer groups, even when she was invited.

Playing politics or conforming to a group role for peer acceptance might have helped Jennifer develop more friendships and might have spared her from feeling odd, different, and unwanted in the short term. Instead she maintained a Real Self that was not compromised by the shaping of her peers. She was herself, an individual. She did not have to experience judgment from others if she was not willing to follow unfamiliar roles and values. For this, she also felt a sense of pride. In fact, she was envied by peers who followed trends that were shaped by more popular peers in leadership roles who set the standards within the various groups at school.

Within therapy, Jennifer was able to recognize what her own responsibility could be in developing friendships and positive connections with others. She was open to considering compromise as an option, rather than the choices of rejecting others or feeling obligated to behave with self-incongruence. Since one of her therapy goals was to understand the causes of her poor social interactions and short-lasting friendships, the insight about her past chosen behaviors was valued.

Jennifer would not give up her Real Self. Instead, she would try to listen more, rather than feel the need to be heard. She also wanted to be more aware and accepting of other people's values and interests, even when they were different from her own. Lastly, she could restrain from her routinely Honest Self presentations when the audience or timing was not right. This was a matter of choice that might lessen conflicts and possibly open communication up for mutual understanding on various topics.

A Teen's Feelings of Rejection

Ricky was a 15-year-old male who had just returned home from placement at a six-month residential treatment program. His family system was in disarray, his parents were going through a divorce, and he had been acting out through substance abuse, poor school performance, fighting with peers, and arguments at home. He lived primarily with his father, by choice. Ricky struggled with issues of abandonment and recalled that when he was younger, his father was always at work, his mother was emotionally unavailable, and older siblings paid little attention to him. He stated, "They didn't care."

After Ricky was discharged from residential treatment, he entered into outpatient therapy. From the treatment program, he learned to verbalize his feelings appropriately rather than act them out. He also gained awareness into the sources of his acting-out behaviors. One of Ricky's insights addressed experiences of parental neglect that ultimately left him to experience a cycle of rejection. "I'm afraid of being hurt, so I shove people away from getting too close, so I like to be left alone." This made sense to him; it was an interesting insight that he tried to work through.

Ricky's primary family members seemed to be rejecting; his trust for them, as well as others, was low. Ricky also exclaimed, "You don't accept comfort; you comfort yourself." Though this was a relatable insight, Ricky spoke of his awareness in second person, somewhat removing himself from the accompanying feelings. His lack of emotional ownership was a safer way of expressing what should have been stated as "I don't accept comfort; I comfort myself." In reality, his Honest Self would have probably said, "I want to be comforted; I want my parents to comfort me." In therapy, Ricky still struggled to be open with his statements. His Core Self was still guarded around true feelings that might trigger unwanted emotional responses.

Part of what Ricky learned in his treatment program was to express true feelings as an Honest Self. The rewards from this were recognized and processed in treatment. At his placement, he was surrounded by supportive therapists. His peers were also learning the same value that comes from being real and honest. However, Ricky soon learned that the safe environment experienced from his program was actually less welcoming outside of treatment.

Following his discharge from residential treatment, Ricky had difficulty verbalizing his thoughts and feelings freely, since others did not readily respond with care or interest. His tendency was to return to a place where he was more of a safer Hidden Self, though his treatment progress placed him in a position where he was more in tune with being his Real Self. This was true most of the time. Nevertheless, Ricky still needed to learn to trust important people in his life, as well as develop more trust within his outpatient therapy.

Ricky recognized his rejection cycle was contradictory to his Core Self but stated he did this to "avoid being hurt by others." He stated, "I see myself as being caring toward others, yet I push them away." Interestingly, Ricky stated he would push his parents away but realized he "won't do that to my grandparents," who were an important part of his life while growing up. Perhaps with his grandparents, he felt a strong sense of acceptance and freedom to be himself, therefore there was no fear of rejection and no need to protect himself by pushing them away.

When Ricky was in the presence of either of his parents, especially his mother, he felt judged or "under a microscope." Ricky did not feel this way when he was with his grandparents. This was a good example for Ricky to explore. Through this, he had the opportunity to recognize his Core Self. He was then able to be his Real Self, carrying an open mind to feel acceptance from others, while in the process of trying to connect and accept others as well.

Adjusting from Emotional Trauma

Several of my clients have experienced varying levels of trauma from their past. Severe traumas have included such things as physical and sexual assault, being robbed at gunpoint, or experiencing war or natural disasters. These experiences often create anxiety responses that can result in significant maladaptive behaviors as well as depression.

Also consider the clients who have encountered less distressing but consistent or ongoing trauma through such things as verbal and emotional abuse, neglect, or ridicule coming from their childhood and adolescence years. These social/environmental issues often carry lasting emotional effects and may shift the way a person interacts with others. Such experiences can shape a person's style of communication, especially when confronted with similar negative exchanges.

It is challenging for a person to behave as their Core Self when past traumatic experiences emotionally interfere with them, and anxiety or depressive symptoms surface. Part of the treatment of reclaiming the Core Self is recognizing that past negative experiences can unbalance a person to the point that they may become overly guarded or adjust to negative surroundings in an unhealthy way.

Strong emotions can get in the way of a person's ability to express themself safely, so there may be a tendency to display other emotions that are not natural but feel protective. One way we can see this process therapeutically unfold is during Critical Incident Stress Debriefings (CISD). These CISDs are commonly done with first responders or a group of witnesses to traumatic events soon after it has occurred. This CISD process helps to lessen the impact of the trauma through group support, while aiding those present to return to their more normal, functioning self.

Within this form of group processing, there can be a qualitative movement from one's feeling state to a cognitive state. This is done within a supportive and caring environment. When processing the event cognitively, one should experience better self-regulation and internal control. Similarly, when working with an individual in psychotherapy, personal emotional experiences may also be explored through a cognitive approach.

When processing issues with clients who have histories of less severe but consistent emotional types of trauma, it can be beneficial to help the client identify the source of their hurt. As previously discussed, this can occur during a phase of therapy when a client feels safe enough to explore past relationships and experiences that have contributed to blocking the natural flow of their Core Self. If they can recognize such contacts and events that had a personal impact in negatively shifting positions of the Self, they may openly address the information from retrieved memories.

Through this process, a person can move to a better place of being rational; they can examine the Self that was more comfortably accessible and present. Reclaiming the Core Self should open up and release the client toward choosing more real and appropriate relationships. They might then receive responses or actions with others that better match their Real or Honest Self.

Between the various forms of verbal and emotional abuse, a common theme is present. There is a purposeful effort for dominance of power over another. The communication made to the receiver of the power-infused message is that there should be compliance and acceptance. The material conveyed may be outwardly demanding or subtly manipulative for control.

A person in a power position may directly push for something from someone in some way. Here, the receiver of the communication is pressured to behave unnaturally through coercion, withholding, or intimidation. A less obvious but overwhelmingly harmful abusive communication is that of the Double Bind. Here a person, usually in a power position, communicates about something on two separate levels that are contradictory. The receiver of the communication is confused about the contrasting messages but may not comment on their incompatibility due to the power role of the communicator.

Consistent repeated types of such unhealthy exchanges can result in a subconscious acceptance of the dysfunctional communication pattern. Here, the underlying tone of the communication is unbalanced and can become psychologically harmful to the receiver. These patterns tend to pull a person away from their Core Self due to subconscious efforts to get along and cooperate with the communicator. The receiver of mixed messages must sort out the meanings of the contradictory communications and determine how best to respond in a healthy manner.

The process of returning to the Core Self and developing better assertiveness skills is important for clients from families with dysfunctional communication patterns. This action may be an uncomfortable undertaking but the insights may be valuable since they will support one's movement to change. For those who encounter Double Bind messages, adults will have more freedom than children to address incongruity and to change their own thinking and actions. However, change is an arduous shift and requires a person to have confidence with limit-setting behavior. The goal is to develop better clarity of thought and to operate as a Real or Honest Self.

To Fear or Not to Fear

The last example presented relates specifically to anxiety. This emotional issue is frequently approached in therapy and gets precipitated by several different factors. Clients work to understand why they might feel mild nervousness, or in some situations a strong panic response, over simple identifiable items or seemingly benign situations. As it applies to the Core Self, there are certain social interactions that can provoke anxiety and lead to feelings of discomfort and incongruity.

Some examples that commonly trigger anxiety are starting a new job, meeting certain people for the first time, playing an important position for a team of people, or leading a group of peers in a project. Each of these situations can be handled comfortably without fears, however for many, they are often the source of repeated anxiety. Incongruent feelings of the Self may be a primary cause for this discomfort.

One of the most common occasions when anxiety is experienced is through public speaking. The thought of having to be in the spotlight and verbally make some coherent sense of some subject to others can feel overwhelming, even for the most seasoned public speaker. Though it may be simple and comfortable enough for many, it tends to feel overwhelming to others and can even create somatic problems such as stomach pain or headaches.

For some, there is a fear of making mistakes or being ridiculed by the audience. For others, there is self-doubt that makes them question whether they are knowledgeable enough to present as "the expert." Whatever the cognitive distortion may be, excessive thinking interferes with the goal of sharing knowledge or performing comfortably. The key component here is that there is too much focus placed on performance.

It is often the preoccupation of the delivery that creates the uncertainty in ourselves. I personally learned this while at a meeting among colleagues. I was nervous while waiting to be called upon, expecting to make a statement about some issue that I knew and understood extremely well. My heart rate and pulse went higher than usual, while my breathing became shallow, accompanied by a general uneasy feeling. All these feelings occurred in anticipation of being asked to speak. Then I realized that I was struggling to say things that actually mattered to me. Instead of going with a natural articulation of what I knew and could share, I was concerned about presenting well enough and meeting the supposed expectations of my peers.

My aim was to deliver my statements with perfection. This was an easy way to lose my Core Self, thus increasing the dissension between who I am and what I think others think I am. If I played the part, as an actor might do, I might get lucky and please those at the table. If I chose to speak genuinely about a topic I understand, maybe the physical discomforts of anxiety would diminish. Choosing to speak about a subject I knew and could expand upon if necessary was an opportunity to share and be helpful. This was the actual purpose of my speaking. Once I realized there were no other expectations, I became more relaxed and presented as myself.

When clients struggle to comfortably be themselves in various social situations, we can look at their Real Self and how this is a representation of their deeper Core Self. As previously discussed in the case of Sarah, there is value in recalling earlier memories in a person's life history, a time when they felt freer to express themself with lower inhibition. At these times, the client was less likely to feel anxiety. Overthinking with negative thoughts was also less frequent during that time. The impulse to react naturally was more typical and predictable. As was the case of Maggie, there should not be a primary focus on performance standards to accommodate or please others.

The concern over presenting well enough to meet supposed group expectations is a burden that inhibits the Real and Honest Self. Self-acceptance is more important so that the feeling of congruence between "who I am" and "how I present to others" is in agreement. Such harmony within the Self should then be consistent and felt in all areas of a person's life. Regardless of the role one is portraying at a moment in time, their Core Self exists within.

Summary of Approach and Interventions

There is value in maintaining a consistent, genuine Self that is present in all areas of one's life. For example, the roles of one individual could be as a husband, son, brother, friend, coach, musician, writer, and weekend gardener. Each of these personas maintain the internal depth of the Core Self. They are attached with a common connecting thread that should be identifiable and makes us who we are, no matter what role we carry at any particular moment.

This Core Self is within us, and it should never leave a person. Once that familiar core thread is realized, the therapist can help to support and guide a client toward self-discovery. This is achieved through understanding and respecting the unique components of that person's Self. It is up to the client to recognize their core being and stay consistent with their Real Self. They are also able to decide when an Honest Self presentation is beneficial, depending on different social contexts. Clients are encouraged to behave with what is socially appropriate, while being mindful of potential outcomes.

Much of the Honest Self can be expressed in a therapeutic setting. In this environment, there should be a general feeling of safety. The setting is favorable since the therapist communicates to the client with constructive, supportive feedback. Initially in treatment, clients may be guarded and reluctant to share thoughts and feelings. In some cases, they may attempt to present themselves in certain ways to get along with the therapist and to avoid feeling judged. In other situations, clients may subconsciously try to mislead the therapist to avoid self-disclosure and minimize uncomfortable emotions. These false self-presentations may initially be observed with some individuals or couples. This is a defense and is often meant to reduce responsibility for one's own role with the presenting problem.

A false self-presentation is less likely to be observed in family therapy. This is because family members typically enact their family dynamics more accurately and are more likely to confront fake presentations from family members within therapy sessions. Of course, all this is based upon the unique characteristics of each particular family system and the individuals within it.

Family members at all age levels will likely know Core Self components for each individual. With an engaged family system that is interacting, they may need to be encouraged or will naturally address each other's natural temperament. Under these conditions, the therapist may enter into the family system and guide them toward honest expression. Eventually, most clients will reveal themselves in therapy. This may be achieved through individual, couples, and family therapy.

Unedited self-expression can be seen in certain nontherapeutic relationships such as work, group organizations, and longtime friendships. This occurs because trust with others may be earned over time. After multiple communication exchanges, people tend to behave less guardedly and reveal parts of themselves with more openness, such as within most family systems. Ultimately within a therapeutic setting, the client reveals their Core Self; this should progress over time due to increased comfort.

The basic elements supporting a Real or Honest Self presentation in therapy relate to increased trust over time and the comfort provided in the therapeutic setting. These are both instrumental in establishing a safe and authentic therapeutic relationship. There is increased security felt as the therapist promotes the value that comes from being real and honest. No judgment should be felt, and there should be no necessitated push for a client's expression. Instead, the therapist gently pulls for such genuine affect. The pace of openness is based on what the client is comfortable sharing. They set their own rate of disclosure. The therapist's function is to help facilitate the client's potential to be real while developing self-acceptance.

Revealing one's Self in therapy is an emotional process. Being honest with thoughts and feelings through the therapeutic process can feel risky. Therefore, it is important to recognize the responsibility a therapist has for guiding clients toward a healthier emotional place. Due to the client's vulnerability, therapists must be sensitive and recognize the importance of feelings. The insights acquired through therapy are beneficial, but the associated emotions may increase resistance and avoidance. This is why we do not push for emotional responses from personal life events.

There is a sensitivity within the client that may need supportive feedback. Under the right conditions, the client will verbalize their experiences, sometimes through an emotional recall and other times with a less expressive acknowledgment. Regardless of the presentation, the therapist is responsible for helping the client make sense of their realization. The next part of the process is to work toward an understanding of the Real Self and use therapy to practice Honest Self disclosures.

The vignettes presented in this chapter demonstrate examples of appropriate pacing for clients in a therapeutic setting. With each case there is a significant amount of safety, giving comfort to the client and bringing them to a level of openness and honesty. The process of therapy can be direct and more short term, or it may become a longer journey. This may depend on the level of incongruity within the Self that exists for the client at the time they enter treatment. What mode of the Self does the person typically operate in? Are they open to exploring their Core Self and behave as a Real Self?

It is important to realize that a person's feelings of incongruity may have been present for a long time, which may also mean their tendency to behave as a Lost or Hidden Self has become automatic and dysfunctionally comfortable. It is what the person knows and therefore it becomes difficult for them to see their false presentation as a problem. An important role of the therapist is to help clients recognize alternative ways to interact with others in a healthier manner. Clients should strive to recognize who they are as their Core Self, thus accepting the elements of the Self that define who they are.

Ultimately, this mode of therapy aims to help people accept and understand their Core Selves. It encourages openness and self-acceptance, and helps people embrace who they are. The goal is to help people reach a place where they feel confident and open to new possibilities. Recognizing and appreciating the Core Self is useful for gaining a deeper understanding of who we are.

Chapter 10

Benefits of Self-Acceptance

It is important to acknowledge certain pioneers in humanistic psychology who have shared similar views to Core Self Theory regarding human nature. The humanistic view emphasizes the importance of being authentically oneself. Carl Rogers and Abraham Maslow recognized the value of this, which is described in their models. Each has highlighted the importance of personal growth through self-discovery and the need for authenticity and achieving self-actualization.

Humanistic theories have sought to support and encourage a person's unique individual differences from others with an emphasis on the freedom to be one's self. Within such models, an important aspiration is to experience self-actualization. It is an individual's inclination to engage in the ongoing process of self-understanding that focuses on self-fulfillment with a healthy self-concept. When we strive toward self-actualization, we are working on meeting our own potential. We do this while being authentic.

Similar to Person-Centered Therapy, this model recognizes the importance of vulnerability when experiencing incongruent feelings. According to Rogers, this may occur when a client recognizes a discrepancy between what they are feeling and how they present themself to the outside. In Core Self Theory, the client is challenged to explore the deeper components that define their Core Self and recognize more authentic reactions to personal and social situations. When we are not authentic, we are disingenuous and likely to feel the emotional impact of incongruence. As a result of this incongruity, we are more likely to develop symptoms of anxiety and depression.

One of the key components that sets Core Self Theory apart from other humanistic models is the therapeutic process designed to help clients become their Real and Honest Selves. Self-discovery is beneficial, and sorting out issues that prevent an individual from being a Real or Honest Self are significant. One can internally explore their own levels of authenticity through introspection, but also accepting the guidance of a skilled professional through insights may be rewarding. Addressing difficult questions posed by a therapist may also aid with the process of self-discovery. The other important feature in this process is the acknowledgment that there is a Core Self, unique and separate from all other individuals. Acceptance through appreciating the elements of the Core Self is less about genetics and social shaping and more about something internal and spiritual.

The advantages of accepting one's Core Self can be felt on a personal level as well as on a social one. Welcoming the elements of ourselves without resistance benefits us, since it permits us to think, feel, and behave in ways that are most natural instead of false. From the very beginning of our lives, we are unique individuals. As each of us moves forward in our lives, we have ongoing experiences that contribute to our personality development. Being who we are is an accomplishment in self-acceptance and ideally will prompt our acceptance of others.

Recognizing our own deeper, personal feelings and accepting them as our own can sometimes feel overwhelming and challenging, especially when our internal experience seems different or separate from others. At times we are comfortably aligned with the people we are engaged with, yet at other times we experience discomfort and unease. In these moments of personal difference, the simplicity of accepting a group mentality as our own may seemingly reduce the complexities that might arise from individuality, however the chance of rising internal discomfort is more likely.

Incongruence of the Self will occur when an individual denies, avoids, or minimizes their personal experience within a given situation. When we try to accept and adopt a viewpoint that is not our own, feelings of discomfort may occur and ultimately increase stress. Acknowledging the concepts of the Lost Self and Hidden Self are paths to understanding this phenomena. If a pattern of denying Core Self reactions exists and continues, an individual is more likely to experience depressive symptoms or various levels of anxiousness.

This is a model of self-acceptance and is meant to encourage individuals to recognize who they truly are and appreciate what they actually think and feel. In turn, they will react/respond to situations that match who they are and are congruent to their natural selves. When this is consistent, the Real Self and Honest Self will emerge. A more congruent Self is not going to encounter the internal conflicts experienced by someone who conceals their personal views and opinions. Granted, one may not always be appreciated for expressing unpopular views, but there may be a personal gratification that overcomes the discomfort felt from withholding one's own truth.

Allowing yourself to truly be who you are is a gift that opens up the Self to other benefits. The value of self-acceptance helps to develop a better and more accurate self-image. When we know, like, and accept who we are, we will have improved self-esteem and increased confidence. It may require strength to present oneself in ways that do not easily match the norms of a dominant group, but choosing to be real or honest has its own rewards that should not be minimized.

It is hard to explore the needs of others until we are able to accept and embrace our own needs. In other words, I must first understand myself. I am literally the center of the universe, that is to say, my own universe. Where I stand is the ultimate center, and everything around me is outside of myself. Where each of us stands is symbolically our own single world. Everything moves outward, bit by bit. It is unique and centered from my inner-mind's eye, then moves outward to the rest of the universe. Self-acceptance is not only understanding who I am but also appreciating my unique individuality.

Beyond self-acceptance, the next goal is to improve our relations with other people. This significant improvement made for the Self is likely to expand to others, especially those who also reveal themselves openly. Mutual acceptance is an ideal. Sharing support for one another's view, opinions, and ideas will not actually mean agreeability. It simply indicates there is respect given through the acceptance of another person's Core Self beliefs. Our objective is not to change others or convince them to see things as we do. We can have the freedom to mutually share among each other in our relationships. Being in a position of nonjudgmental acceptance is to see a person for who they are. Reciprocating can denote openness and respect for another. Such a response demonstrates a willingness to listen. It is a gesture that is encouraging to others and frees us to express ourselves more openly.

On a larger scale, the value of acceptance for Self and others may be applied to children in the school setting. Some schools have already added into their curriculum certain versions of teaching this concept. Imagine the positivity that can emerge when teachers and counselors are consistent with such mantras as "be yourself" and "accept others just as you would like to be accepted." Some studies have created school programs to teach students peer support of fellow students. Other school programs encourage students to accept each other despite personal limitations or disabilities. An example of this relates to schools that have bullying intervention programs.

There is value in pairing different types of students with the goal of engaging them. Through this process, students learn cooperative skills and develop an appreciation of each other's differences. Sometimes this is done by creating a "buddy system," while others might be in a role as a tutor. The Jigsaw Classroom is another example of increasing peer connectedness. Through this method, students experience a cooperative learning technique as a means of promoting student interdependence while in pursuit of a common goal. They are divided into groups, each group specializing in a specific component of a larger project. Students become dependent on each other for success in the overall project. Here, cooperative skills become the valued behavior, and students are more supportive during the learning process.

Teachers may include basic principles of the Core Self through demonstrating and encouraging appropriate peer interactions. Teachers can promote the ideals of the model by reinforcing the general concepts of acceptance and honest communication. Here, the goal is to help children accept their identity as well as accept the uniqueness of others. After all, why have most teachers chosen to enter the field of education? Likely, it was not solely to teach ABCs and 123s. They entered their field more likely for altruistic reasons, such as positively influencing young minds for the future. An additional objective should be to teach a humanistic approach of helping children to be happier as themselves.

Parents should certainly be at the heart of communicating these values. They should be encouraged to support their children with self-acceptance as well as acceptance of others. Raising children with appropriate Core Self values means recognizing their temperaments as well as the other unique qualities that separate them from other children. It is good to acknowledge their emotions and support children to talk about their feelings. The opportunity to share feelings without parental judgment creates a safer environment for future disclosures and openness with emotions.

In conclusion, the value of gaining self-understanding and accepting who we are can be beneficial to oneself and others. This includes all ages. Actively being our Core Self enables us to think more naturally and behave more authentically. With this approach to life, we are likely to feel the freedom to think and feel in a most natural manner. Once we have Core Self insight, we will carry an awareness enabling us to choose the proper self-state that matches the best communication needed at the moment.

Through Core Self Theory, individuals are encouraged to accept themselves as unique human beings. Through the different applications of personal growth, social connectedness, and insight for deeper self-understanding, acceptance of Self and others is essential. The deep inner self is constantly within us, yet for some it is buried and difficult to access. This is because it involves internal genuine feelings that may have been shaped by others who are less accepting. Remember, knowing your Core Self and allowing it to exist naturally may be one of the best gifts you give yourself. Your Core Self is who you were, are, and will always be.

Within each of us is a safe harbor where we once dwelt happily, no matter how stormy the world was around us. We knew what we liked, what we did not like, what we wanted, what we did not want, and how to stand up for our rights. Eventually, through many outside forces, we learned to express them less and less, even to ourselves. Some of us became Lost Selves and completely forgot who we truly are, some remained true to themselves, but their honesty caused them many difficulties and resistance from others.

This model of the Core Self urges us to become reacquainted with ourselves and to navigate who we are in the world in an authentic manner and in our own unique ways. There are times when it would be beneficial for us and for others to curb our Honest Self from expressing itself freely for the sake of social harmony, but what joy it is to do so with our own volition, our own decision, and our own will.

This Core Self Theory aims at empowering each one of us with the realization that within us still lies the miracle birth of the unique person we have always been.

Articles and
Books of Related Interest

Adler, Alfred. 1930. *The Education of Children*, translated by Eleanore and Friedrich Jansen. George Allen & Unwin Limited.

Dreikurs, Rudolf, and Vicki Stolz. 1991. *Children: The Challenge, the Classic Work on Improving Parent–Child Relations—Intelligent, Humane, and Eminently Practical*. Plume.

Maslow, Abraham H. 1962. *Toward a Psychology of Being*. D. Van Nostrand.

Rogers, Carl R. 1942. *Counseling and Psychotherapy*. Houghton Mifflin.

Saroyan, John. 2021. "Developing a Supportive Peer Environment: Engaging Students through Cooperative Skills in the Classroom." *Advances in Developmental and Educational Psychology* 3 (1), 81-89. https://doi.org/10.25082/ADEP.2021.01.001.

Saroyan, John. 2019. "Bullying Affects the Core Self of Children." *Peace Review* 31 (1): 24–33. doi:10.1080/10402659.2019.1613592.

Thomas, Alexander, and Stella Chess. 1986. "The New York Longitudinal Study: From Infancy to Early Adult Life." In *The Study of Temperament*, edited by Robert Plomin and Judith Dunn. Psychology Press.

Watzlawick, Paul, Janet Beavin Bavelas, and Don D. Jackson. 2011. *Pragmatics of Human Communication: A Study of Interactional Patterns, Pathologies and Paradoxes*. W. W. Norton.

Acknowledgments

I am grateful and indebted to those who have supported me in the process of moving this book from a mere idea to an actual completed project. Though my parents are long deceased, I would like to acknowledge them for having impressed upon me their values and independent spirits. Thank you to my children, Lynn, Danielle, and Anthony, for your continuous love and support during this writing process. A special thanks to my childhood friend Eric Noel Muñoz who aptly recommended Transformation Media Books. I also want to thank Dr. Nivla Fitzpatrick for her support, as well as Pamela Riss and Carmen Anderson for their assistance during the final stages of writing this book. Thank you to Susan Swartwout for her care during the final process in this publishing endeavor. Lastly, I want to thank Jennifer Geist, my publisher, for making this experience, from beginning to end, a pleasant and effective journey.

About the Author

John Saroyan, EdD, received his doctorate in counseling and educational psychology at the University of San Francisco. He is a licensed clinical psychologist and licensed marriage and family therapist, with a private practice in San Pedro, California. He is also a psychologist at the Pepperdine University Counseling Center in Malibu, California. As a Fulbright Scholar Specialist, Dr. Saroyan helped develop mental health treatment programs for children and adolescents outside the country. As a military and family life consultant with the United States Department of Defense, he worked with American soldiers and their families internationally.

Dr. Saroyan has published articles related to *Core Self Theory* and coauthored *Trapped Between Innocence and Death*, a book addressing the complexities of gang culture. As the clinical director of adolescent treatment programs in Los Angeles County, he played a pivotal role in shaping the futures of at-risk youth. Beyond his professional accomplishments, Dr. Saroyan enjoys spending time with his family, playing music, and traveling.